OCEANS AND RIVERS
STICKER-PEDIA

Silver Dolphin

San Diego, California

Silver Dolphin

Silver Dolphin Books
An imprint of the Advantage Publishers Group
5880 Oberlin Drive, San Diego, CA 92121-4794
www.silverdolphinbooks.com

Author: Jinny Johnson

Copyright © Marshall Editions, 2003

A Marshall Edition
Conceived, edited, and designed by Marshall Editions
The Old Brewery, 6 Blundell Street, London N7 9BH, U.K.
www.quarto.com

ISBN 1-59223-047-4

1 2 3 4 5 07 06 05 04 03

Originated in Singapore by Universal Graphics
Printed and bound in China by CT Printing
Design: Ian Bayliss and Roger Christian
Copyediting: Mary-Jane Wilkins and Andrew Mackay

The access code for your CD-ROM is:
SHARK

Contents

How to use
this book   6

Below the surface   8

Story Pages
  What is a fish?   10
Animal Pages   12
Story Pages
  Sharks   18
Play Pages
  Coral reef   28
Animal Pages   30
Story Pages
  Tuna   40
Animal Pages   42

Play Pages
  Freshwater   48
Animal Pages   50
Play Pages
  Deep-sea   64
Animal Pages   66
Story Pages
  Mollusks   72
Animal Pages   74

Above the surface 82

Animal Pages 84
Story Pages
   Antarctic seals 86
Animal Pages 88
Play Pages
   Beach 96
Animal Pages 98
Story Pages
   Nile crocodiles 100
Animal Pages 102
Play Pages
   Pond 112
Animal Pages 114

Glossary 122
List of animals 123
Acknowledgments 128

STICKER SHEETS **129**
Animal Pages Stickers
   Below the surface 129
   Above the surface 145
Play Pages Stickers 155

How to use this book

This Sticker-pedia has two parts. In the first part we introduce you to animals that live below the surface of the oceans. The second part is all about animals that rely on water but also spend part of their lives on land.

On the Animal Pages you can add the stickers that are found at the back of this book. You can also read some fascinating facts about each animal.

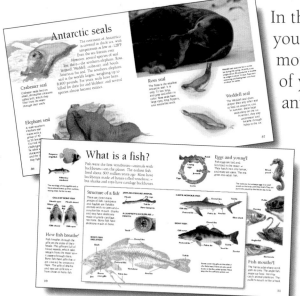

In the Story Pages you can discover more about some of your favorite animals, such as sharks and seals.

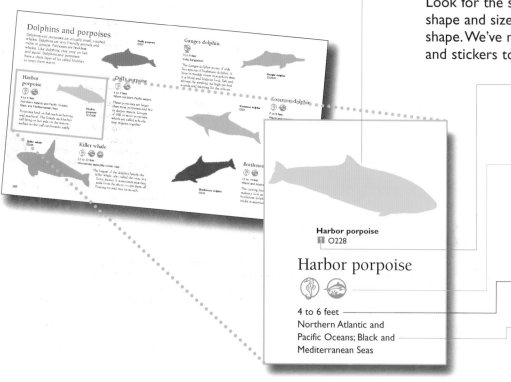

Sticker shape
This is where you put your stickers. Look for the sticker that matches the shape and size of the colored animal shape. We've numbered all the animals and stickers to help you match them up.

Extinction warning!
This symbol tells you that the animal is in danger of dying out.

Habitat
These symbols show you what sort of environment this animal lives in. These symbols are explained on the next page.

Size
The length of the animal.

Range
The regions in which this animal is found.

You can have even more sticker fun with the Play Pages. Try arranging your stickers in the different watery scenes.

Coral reef play page

You can find the stickers of fish that live on tropical reefs on page 155. Stick them on this page to create your own coral reef scene.

You'll find all your stickers at the back of the book. The ones for the Animal Pages are on pages 129 to 154. The stickers for the Play Pages are on pages 155 to 160. Start sticking!

Key to habitat symbols

 Deep sea
Deep, dark seawater far beneath the surface

 Coast
Land bordering the sea: mud flats, shores, cliffs, islands, and tidal areas

 Coastal water
Seawater close to land: estuaries and the seabed

 Coral reef
A rocklike ridge or reef in the sea, made up of coral and other organic material

 Oceanic
Open seas and oceans: top and middle layers of water

 Freshwater
Inland water: rivers, lakes, ponds, lagoons, streams, wetlands, marshes, swamps, floodplains, springs, ditches, dams, riverbanks, and underground water in caves

 Temperate grassland
Open country in areas with a mild climate: steppes, prairies, the bush, moors, and lowlands

 Tropical grassland
Open country in areas with a hot climate: savannas

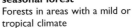 **Deciduous forest and seasonal forest**
Forests in areas with a mild or tropical climate

 Tropical evergreen forest
Forests in hot regions: rain forests and mangroves

 Inhabited areas and agricultural land
Areas close to where people live: gardens, orchards, parks, farmland, towns and cities, hedgerows, and roadsides

 Tundra and polar
Icy regions: the Antarctic and Arctic

 Desert
Desertlike areas in hot regions: rocky areas, sandy areas, semidesert, scrubs, brushlands, and very dry land

7

Below the surface

There are more than 24,000 species of fish in the world, all living below the surface of oceans, rivers, and lakes. Tiny species, such as the pygmy goby, are just one-third of an inch long, but giants such as the whale shark can measure as much as 40 feet.

In addition to fish, there is also a huge range of invertebrates (creatures without a backbone) living in our seas. About a million species of invertebrate animals, including crabs, clams, and jellyfish, live in every part of the ocean. Some mammals, such as whales and dolphins, also live in the oceans. Unlike fish, they have no gills, so they have to come to the surface regularly to breathe air.

These bluestripe snappers swim in a large group called a school, or shoal. A school of fish can confuse predators by turning and changing direction very fast.

Lionfish

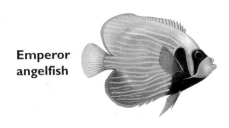

Emperor angelfish

Atlantic mackerel

The markings of the angelfish and the mackerel break up their outlines, making them harder to see.

GILLS OF BONY FISH

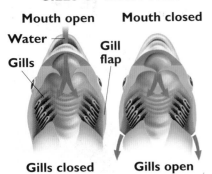

Mouth open   Mouth closed

Water

Gill flap

Gills

Gills closed   Gills open

How fish breathe

Fish breathe through the gills on the sides of their heads. The gills are full of blood vessels, which take oxygen from the water as it passes through them. Bony fish have gills that are covered by protective flaps. The gills of sharks and rays are different from those of bony fish.

What is a fish?

Fish were the first vertebrates—animals with backbones—on the planet. The earliest fish lived about 500 million years ago. Most have backbones made of bones called vertebrae, but sharks and rays have cartilage backbones.

Structure of a fish

There are three main groups of fish. Lampreys and hagfish are fishlike animals with no jaws and a suckerlike mouth. Sharks and rays have skeletons made of gristly cartilage, not bone. Bony fish have skeletons made of bone.

JAWLESS FISHLIKE ANIMAL

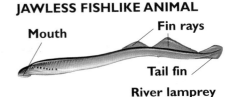

Mouth

Fin rays

Tail fin

River lamprey

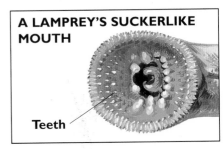

A LAMPREY'S SUCKERLIKE MOUTH

Teeth

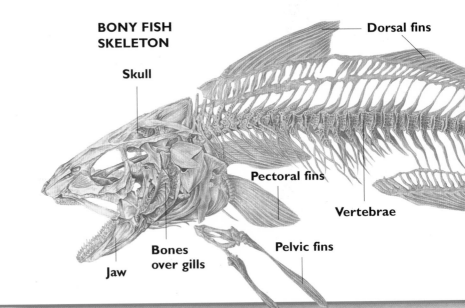

BONY FISH SKELETON

Dorsal fins

Skull

Pectoral fins

Vertebrae

Jaw

Bones over gills

Pelvic fins

Eggs and young

Fish eggs are laid and fertilized in the water. They hatch into tiny larvae, and many are eaten. The rest grow into adult fish.

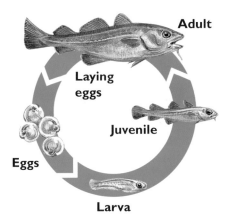

Adult

Laying eggs

Juvenile

Eggs

Larva

Brood pouch

The male sea horse keeps eggs in a small pouch on his body until they hatch. They are put in the pouch by the female sea horse.

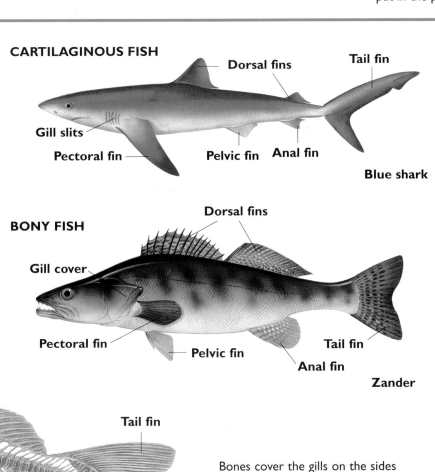

CARTILAGINOUS FISH

Dorsal fins

Tail fin

Gill slits

Pectoral fin

Pelvic fin

Anal fin

Blue shark

BONY FISH

Dorsal fins

Gill cover

Pectoral fin

Pelvic fin

Tail fin

Anal fin

Zander

Tail fin

Anal fin

Bones cover the gills on the sides of a fish's head. There are also small bones in the fins, called spines. These keep the fins stiff and spread out.

Puffer

Herring

Anglerfish

Barracuda

Fish mouths

The barracuda's sharp teeth grab its prey. The anglerfish snaps up food. Herring catch animal plankton. The puffer's mouth is like a beak.

Hagfish, lampreys, skates, and rays

Hagfish and lampreys are fishlike animals that do not have true jaws. They don't bite their food, but bore into it or suck it up. Skates and rays are diamond-shaped, with a broad, flat body and huge, winglike fins. As they swim, they flap their fins up and down, so they look as if they are flying through the water.

Skate
01

Skate

8 feet
Eastern Atlantic Ocean;
Arctic Ocean to Madeira;
Mediterranean Sea

The skate has a flat body, broad fins, and a tiny tail with small spines on it. Skates eat fish, crabs, lobsters, and octopuses.

Southern stingray

5 feet wide
Atlantic coast: New
Jersey to Brazil; Gulf
of Mexico; Caribbean

Stingrays have long, thin tails and are almost rectangular. They have a sharp spine near the tail, which can poison an attacker and could kill a human.

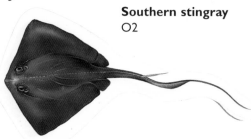

Southern stingray
02

Electric ray
03

Electric ray

6 feet
Atlantic Ocean: Scotland to South Africa, Nova
Scotia to North Carolina; Mediterranean Sea

Electric rays can give electric shocks strong enough to kill or stun their prey or cause injury to a human.

Greater sawfish

25½ feet
Temperate and tropical oceans

The greater sawfish has a long, bladelike snout studded with 24 or more teeth on each side. It lives on the seabed in shallow water and uses its saw to dig in the sand and mud for small invertebrates to eat.

Greater sawfish
O4

Atlantic manta ray
O5

Atlantic manta ray

17 feet long; 22 feet wide
Atlantic Ocean

The manta is the biggest of the rays. It feeds mostly on tiny animal plankton, which it filters from the water.

Atlantic hagfish
O6

Atlantic hagfish

24 inches
Arctic Ocean; North
Atlantic Ocean

The hagfish has no jaws, just a slitlike mouth surrounded by small tentacles. It feeds on crustaceans, but it also eats dead and dying fish.

Sea lamprey
O7

Sea lamprey

35½ inches
Mediterranean Sea; Atlantic
Ocean; larvae live in freshwater

The sea lamprey has no jaws and uses its sucking, disklike mouth to attach itself to its prey and suck its blood.

13

Sharks

Sharks are cartilaginous fish, which means their skeleton is made from cartilage instead of bone. All sharks live in the sea and most are active hunters, equipped with sharp-edged teeth.

Port Jackson shark
O8

Port Jackson shark

Up to 5 feet
South Pacific Ocean; Southern Ocean: coasts of Australia from south Queensland to southwestern Australia

The Port Jackson shark is a bullhead shark and has a large, heavy head with a small mouth. It is grayish-brown in color.

Thresher shark
O9

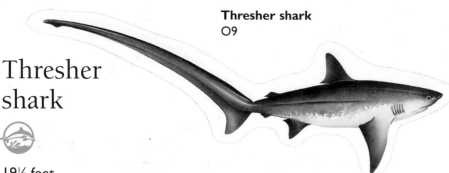

Thresher shark

19½ feet
Temperate and tropical oceans

The tail of a thresher shark is as long as the rest of its body. The sharks lash their tails to herd together the fish they eat, so that they can catch them more easily.

Mako

10 to 13 feet
Atlantic, Pacific, and Indian Oceans: warm and tropical areas

The mako is a powerful shark, colored deep blue on top and white underneath. It is known for its habit of leaping clear of the water.

Basking shark
O10

Basking shark

34 feet
Worldwide, outside the tropics

The basking shark feeds on plankton that it catches by swimming along with its mouth open. The plankton it takes in are sieved from the water through comblike bristles on its gills.

White shark

20 feet
Atlantic, Pacific, and Indian
Oceans: warm and tropical
coastal areas

The white shark ranges in color from
gray to brown with white undersides.
It has often attacked humans.

Sandy dogfish

23 inches to 4 feet
North Atlantic Ocean: coasts
of Norway, Britain, Europe, and
North Africa; Mediterranean Sea

The sandy dogfish is sandy-
brown in color and is
marked with dark brown
spots. It lives on the seabed
and eats fish.

Wobbegong

10 feet
Australia; coastal reefs of the Pacific Ocean

The wobbegong has wormlike
bristles sticking out around its
mouth. It uses these to suck prey
into its razor-sharp teeth.

White shark
O12

Smooth
hammerhead

14 feet
Atlantic, Pacific, and Indian Oceans:
warm and tropical areas

This shark feeds on fish,
especially rays. Hammerheads
are aggressive sharks and have
attacked humans.

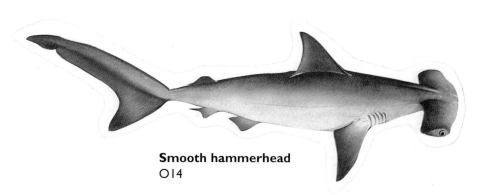

Sandy dogfish
O13

Smooth hammerhead
O14

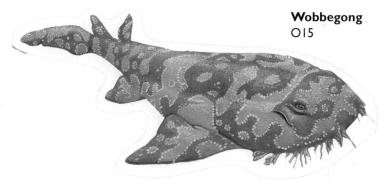

Wobbegong
O15

Nurse shark

2 to 13 feet
Western Atlantic Ocean; eastern Pacific Ocean

The nurse shark has lots of short, sharp teeth, ideal for crushing shellfish. It has whiskers on its flattened head, which help it find hidden prey on the seabed. If disturbed, it tends to crawl, rather than swim, away.

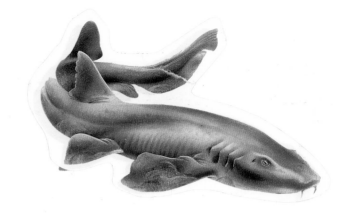

Nurse shark
O16

Horn shark

Up to 4 feet
Eastern coast of Australia

This shark gets its name from the sharp spines in front of the fins on its back. It feeds at night on sea urchins, crabs, and worms from the seabed. It crushes hard-shelled food with its large, flat teeth.

Horn shark
O17

Whale shark

50 feet
All tropical seas

This shark is the largest living fish and can grow up to 60 feet long. It eats small fish and plankton, which it catches by opening its mouth to take in a rush of water. The water flows out through the shark's gills and leaves the plankton for the shark to eat.

Whale shark
O18

16

Bluntnose six-gilled shark

Bluntnose six-gilled shark
O19

6 to 17 feet
Atlantic, Pacific, and Indian Oceans:
warm and temperate areas

This shark feeds on rays and crustaceans.
After mating, the eggs hatch inside the
mother, and the young are 18 to 24 inches
long when they are born.

Common saw shark
O20

Common saw shark

4 feet
South Indian and Pacific Oceans

The common saw shark probes the seabed
with its saw, searching for invertebrates and
bottom-living fish to eat. It has both large
and small teeth along its bladelike snout.

Monkfish
O21

Monkfish

6 feet
North Sea; eastern Atlantic
Ocean: Scotland to North Africa;
Mediterranean Sea

The monkfish often lies
buried in sand or mud,
although it can swim well.
It feeds on flatfish, rays, crabs,
and mollusks. Its young are
born live after the eggs hatch
inside the mother.

Greenland shark

Greenland shark
O22

21 feet
North Atlantic Ocean: inside the Arctic Circle,
south to Gulf of Maine and Britain

The Greenland shark feeds on fish, mollusks,
crustaceans, and squid, as well as on seals,
porpoises, and seabirds. Female sharks
usually give birth to about ten live young.

Sharks

Sharks are found all over the oceans of the world—everywhere from shallow coastal waters to the deepest oceans. The blacktip reef shark can swim in just one foot of water to hunt above a coral reef, while the Portuguese shark can be found more than two miles down, making it one of the deepest-living sharks.

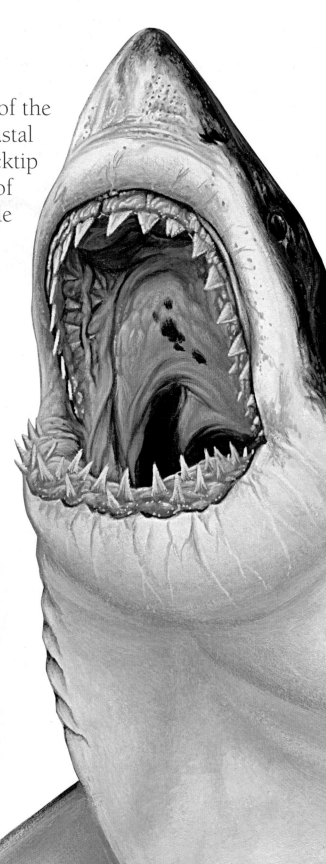

Teeth

Shark teeth come in many shapes and sizes. The teeth of each shark are shaped to help it catch and eat its prey quickly and easily.

The teeth of the mako shark are long and thin and very sharp. They are designed for catching slippery fish.

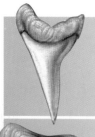

The bronze whaler shark has narrow, jagged-edged teeth that are perfect for catching and gripping its prey.

Horn sharks have pointed teeth at the front to catch small fish, and large, flat teeth at the back to crush sea urchins.

Breathing underwater

It is within the gills that oxygen is taken in from the sea. Blood vessels carry oxygen-rich blood from the gills to the rest of the body. Many hunting sharks must keep swimming to pass the oxygen-rich water over their gills. If they stop, they will sink and drown. Some bottom-dwelling sharks are able to rest on the seabed by pumping water over their gills.

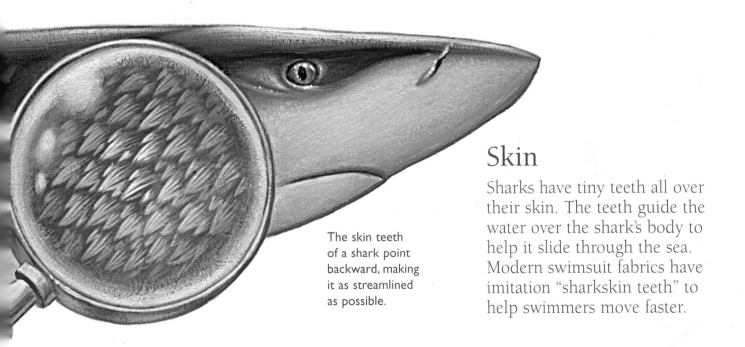

The skin teeth of a shark point backward, making it as streamlined as possible.

Skin

Sharks have tiny teeth all over their skin. The teeth guide the water over the shark's body to help it slide through the sea. Modern swimsuit fabrics have imitation "sharkskin teeth" to help swimmers move faster.

Sturgeons, gars, and relatives

These fish all live in freshwater, except for adult sturgeons, which live in the sea. Sturgeons actually lay their eggs in rivers, where the young stay for several years. Sturgeons are rare, partly because people kill the females and eat their eggs as a food called caviar. Gars, bichirs, and bowfins live where there are a lot of water plants.

Bowfin
O23

Bowfin

36 inches
Northeastern U.S.

This fish lives in slow-moving waters with lots of plants. In spring the male makes a nest in the riverbed. The female lays her eggs and the male guards them for up to ten days, until they hatch.

Bichir
O24

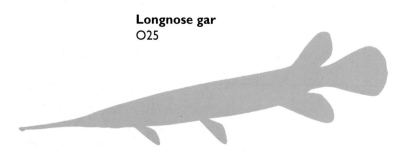

Bichir

16 inches
Central Africa

The bichir has a long body covered with hard, diamond-shaped scales. It lives among water plants at the edges of rivers and lakes. The bichir feeds mainly on fish, frogs, and newts.

Longnose gar
O25

Longnose gar

5 feet
North America

This gar has very long jaws and sharp teeth. It hides among water plants, waiting for fish and shellfish to come near. Then it dashes forward and seizes its prey. The longnose gar lays its eggs in the spring in shallow water.

Elephant-snout fish

32 inches
Nile River

The muscles
along the body of this
fish create a weak electric current around
it. This helps it sense other animals, so it
can find prey at night or in murky water.

Elephant-snout fish
○26

Goldeye
○27

Goldeye

12 to 16 inches
North America

The goldeye has big, golden
eyes and can see well at
night. It has a large number
of small, fine teeth and feeds
on insects.

Pirarucu

Up to 13 feet
South America

The pirarucu can weigh up to 440
pounds. It has large scales on its body but
none on its head. Other fish and insect
larvae are its main food.

Pirarucu
○28

Paddlefish
❗ ○29

Atlantic sturgeon

10 feet
Europe

In the spring,
female sturgeons
lay thousands of
sticky black eggs in
rivers. The young fish stay in the river for
about three years before traveling to the sea.

Atlantic sturgeon
❗ ○30

Paddlefish

6½ feet
Mississippi River and tributaries

The paddlefish swims with
its mouth open and its lower
jaw dropped to catch the
small water creatures it eats.

21

Eels, tarpon, and herring

Most of these fish live in the sea, but some spend time in freshwater. Eels live in all oceans except polar areas. Tarpon are slender sea fish with deeply forked tails. Some herring species, such as sardines and anchovies, are important food fish.

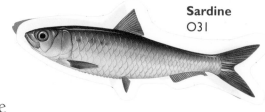

Sardine
O31

Sardine

9¾ inches
Coasts of Europe

Schools of sardines swim in surface waters, feeding on plankton. Large numbers of sardines are caught for food.

Alewife
O32

Alewife

15 inches
Atlantic coast of
North America; northeastern Pacific

The alewife feeds on plankton and small fish. It lives in the sea, but swims into rivers to mate and lay eggs, so is often found in freshwater.

Atlantic herring

15¾ inches
Atlantic and Pacific Oceans

Many herring are caught every year for food. They are also eaten by birds, other fish, dolphins, and seals.

Tarpon

4 to 7¾ feet
Atlantic Ocean

Tarpon
O33

The tarpon is a fast-swimming fish that eats many types of fish and crabs. The female lays millions of eggs in coastal waters. Many of the larvae drift into rivers, where they live until they grow larger.

Atlantic herring
O34

Snipe eel

3¼ to 4 feet
Atlantic, Pacific,
and Indian Oceans

This deep-sea eel has a very long, thin body
with fins along it. It has narrow, beaklike
jaws and sharp, backward-facing teeth to
trap prey such as fish and crustaceans.

Spiny eel
O35

Snipe eel
O36

Spiny eel

4 feet
North Atlantic Ocean

The spiny eel has a long
body with spines on its back
and belly. It eats animals
such as sea anemones.

**Mediterranean
moray**
O37

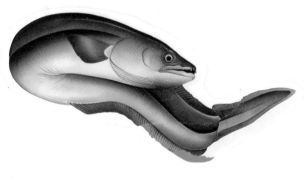

Mediterranean moray

4¼ feet
Northeastern Atlantic; Mediterranean Sea

This moray has a scaleless, patterned body,
powerful jaws, and strong, sharp teeth.
It hides among rocks, watching for prey.

Conger eel

Conger eel
O39

8¾ feet
Coastal waters of the North Atlantic

The conger eel lives in shallow water
on rocky North Atlantic shores. It hides
among rocks and comes out to find fish,
octopus, and other prey.

**European
eel**
O38

European eel

20 to 40 inches
North Atlantic Ocean

When eels are ready to breed, they swim
as far as 3,000 miles out to sea. There
they mate, lay eggs, and then die.

Carp, bream, and piranhas

Carp, bream, roach, and their relatives are freshwater fish. They live in the streams, rivers, and lakes of Europe, northern Asia, and North America and are also found in Africa. Piranhas and pacus belong to a different group of freshwater fish, and most live in Central and South America.

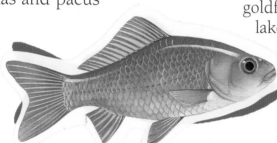

Goldfish

Up to 11¾ inches
Europe and Asia;
introduced worldwide

In the wild, the colorful goldfish lives in ponds and lakes where there are lots of water plants. It is also bred for keeping in aquariums and garden pools.

Goldfish
O40

Red piranha
O41

Red piranha

27½ inches
South America

Piranhas are not large fish, but they swim in such large schools that together they can catch and kill animals much larger than themselves.

Common carp

20 to 40 inches
Southern Europe; introduced into many other areas

The carp is a sturdy fish. It lives in slow-moving water where there is plenty of plant life. It feeds mostly on crustaceans and insect larvae.

Common carp
O42

Pacu
O43

Pacu

Up to 12 inches
Northern South America

The pacu is a peaceful, plant-eating piranha. It feeds on a variety of fruits and seeds that fall from trees along the riverbank.

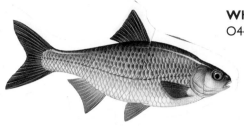

White sucker
O44

Bigmouth
)

White sucker

11¾ to 20½ inches
North America

This bottom-living fish has thick, suckerlike lips, which give it its name. It feeds on insect larvae, crustaceans, mollusks, and plants.

Roach

14 to 18 inches
Europe; western Asia

This river fish eats insects, mollusks, crustaceans, and plants. It, in turn, is food for many fish-eating birds and mammals.

Bigmouth buffalo

3¼ feet
North America

This powerful fish feeds on crustaceans and insect larvae as well as plants. In spring the females lay as many as 500,000 eggs.

Roach
O46

Tench

Up to 27½ inches
Europe; western to central Asia

The tench has a thickset body and rounded fins. It feeds on insect larvae, crustaceans, and mollusks. Tench breed in shallow water, laying their eggs on plants.

Bream

9 to 11 inches
Europe; northern Asia

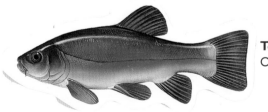

Bream
O47

This fish gathers insect larvae, snails, and worms from the river bottom. It lives in schools and usually feeds at night. Bream breed in shallow water in late spring.

Tench
O48

Catfish and relatives

There are more than 2,400 species of catfish, ranging from tiny fish less than an inch long to giants measuring 5 feet or more. Most live in rivers and freshwater lakes in the warmer parts of the world, but some live in the sea. Many live in South America.

Australian freshwater catfish

23 inches
Southern and eastern Australia

This fish has one fin that runs right around its body. It finds food with the help of whiskers, or barbels, around its mouth.

Surubim

20 to 35 inches
South America

This South American catfish has a long snout and a slender body. The sensitive whiskers, or barbels, around its mouth help it find food.

Surubim
O50

Candirú
O51

Candirú

Up to 2 inches
South America

This tiny, delicate catfish is also called the carnerd. It lives on the blood of other fish. It is usually active at night and buries itself in the riverbed when not feeding.

Cascarudo

7 inches
Tropical South America

The body of this little catfish is covered with overlapping bony plates, which help protect it from enemies.

Cascarudo
O52

Glass catfish

4 inches
Malaysia; Indonesia

This fish is transparent, so you can see many of its internal organs inside its body. It has become a popular species with aquarium owners.

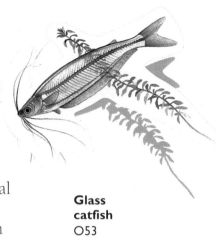

Glass catfish O53

Blue catfish

5 feet
U.S.; Mexico

The blue catfish is one of the largest catfish in North America and can grow to more than 100 pounds. It often lives in fast-moving water, and is even found in rapids and waterfalls.

Blue catfish O55

Sea catfish

12 inches
Western Atlantic Ocean

This sea-living catfish feeds on crabs, shrimp, and fish. When its eggs are laid, the male takes them in his mouth, where they incubate. He cannot eat during this time.

Sea catfish O56

Walking catfish

12 inches
India; Sri Lanka; Southeast Asia; introduced into U.S.

This catfish can live in ponds that dry up often. It can move to another pond by making snakelike movements with its body and using its fins.

Walking catfish O54

Wels

3¼ to 10 feet
Central and eastern Europe

The wels lives in slow-moving water and is active at night. Fish are its main food, but it also eats frogs, birds, and small mammals

Wels O57

Coral reef play page

You can find the stickers of fish that live on tropical reefs on page 155. Stick them on this page to create your own coral reef scene.

Electric eel, salmon, and pike

The electric eel is not a true eel, but it has a similar long body. It is the only species in its family. There are 76 species of salmon, which live both in freshwater and the sea. Pike are a small group of freshwater fish.

Northern pike

5 feet
Northern Europe; Russia; Alaska; Canada; northern U.S.

The pike lurks among plants, keeping watch for prey. Adult pike catch other fish and even birds and small mammals. Female pike are larger than males and can weigh 50 pounds.

Northern pike
O58

Electric eel
O59

Electric eel

7¾ feet
South America

The electric eel can release electric charges into the water. It uses the shocks to kill fish to eat, or to defend itself from enemies. The charge is strong enough to give a human a severe shock.

Smelt

12 inches
North Atlantic Ocean

Smelt live in the sea but breed in freshwater. Adults travel up rivers, where the females lay their eggs on gravel on the riverbed. When they are large enough, the young fish swim to the sea.

Smelt
O60

Grayling

18 inches
Northern Europe

The grayling has a fin like a sail on its back and a forked tail. It eats insects and their larvae, as well as crustaceans and mollusks.

Sockeye salmon
O61

Grayling
O62

Sockeye salmon

33 inches
Pacific Ocean

When they breed, sockeye salmon swim many miles inland to the river where they were hatched.

Rainbow trout

Rainbow
trout
O63

Up to 3¼ feet
Western North America; introduced worldwide

Rainbow trout is an important food fish that is often farmed. In the wild, rainbow trout live in rivers.

Arctic char

10 to 38 inches
Arctic and North Atlantic Oceans

Arctic char spend most of their lives in polar seas, feeding on fish and mollusks. They travel to rivers to breed.

Arctic char
O65

Atlantic salmon

Up to 5 feet
North Atlantic Ocean

The Atlantic salmon swims into rivers to breed. The female makes a shallow nest on the riverbed for her eggs.

Atlantic salmon
O64

31

Cod and ophidiiformes

The cod group includes some of the most popular of all food fish, such as Atlantic cod and haddock. Cod hunt for their food, preying on other fish and invertebrates. Cusk eels and pearlfish are ophidiiformes, which are eellike fish with long tails.

New Providence cusk eel

4 inches
Bahamas

This little eellike fish was discovered in 1967. Other cusk eels live in the deep ocean or in caves.

Rough-head grenadier

35 to 40 inches
North Atlantic Ocean

This is a deep-sea fish with a large head and a tapering tail. Males make loud sounds by vibrating their bladder.

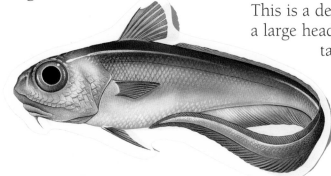

Rough-head
grenadier
O66

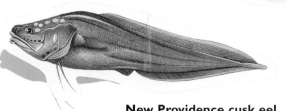

New Providence cusk eel
⚠ O67

Burbot

20 to 40 inches
Canada; northern U.S.; northern Europe; Asia

The burbot is a freshwater fish that hides among water plants by day and comes out at dawn and dusk to feed.

Burbot
O68

Ling

5 to 6½ feet
Northeastern Atlantic Ocean

The ling lives in deep ocean waters, where it eats fish and large crustaceans. It also lives in shallower rocky areas.

Ling
O69

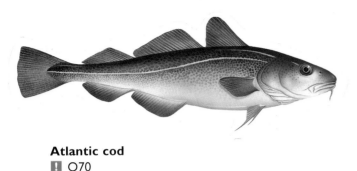

Atlantic cod
 O70

Atlantic cod

4 feet
North Atlantic Ocean

Cod swim in schools and search for food on the seabed. Cod is a valuable food fish for humans, but fewer cod are caught each year because of overfishing.

Haddock

30 inches
North Atlantic Ocean

The haddock feeds on worms, mollusks, and brittle stars, as well as fish. It gathers in schools to spawn, and its eggs float near the surface until they hatch.

Haddock
O71

Pearlfish

8 inches
Mediterranean and Adriatic Seas

Pearlfish are small and slender, with spotted skin. Many live inside other marine animals such as clams, sea urchins, starfish, sea cucumbers, and pearl oysters.

Walleye pollock
O72

Walleye pollock

35 inches
North Pacific Ocean

The pollock has a long, tapering body with three fins on its back and two on its underside. Its head and mouth are large and it has bigger eyes than most other types of cod.

Pearlfish
O73

33

Anglerfish and stomiiformes

There are about 300 species of anglerfish. They have very wide mouths, filled with rows of sharp teeth. Most have a spine on their head that they use to attract prey. Stomiiformes are deep-sea fish and include hatchetfish and viperfish. They all have long teeth and a light-making organ that they use to attract prey in the dark of the deep ocean.

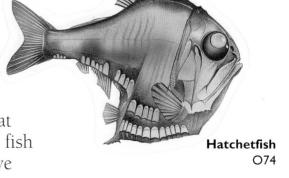

Hatchetfish
O74

Hatchetfish

3 inches
Warm and tropical areas of all oceans

This fish lives in deep water, but comes to the surface at night to find plankton to eat. It has rows of organs on its belly that give out a pale light, confusing predators.

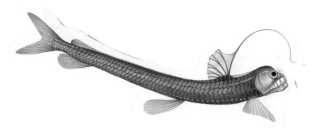

Sloane's viperfish
O75

Sloane's viperfish

12 inches
Atlantic, Pacific, and Indian Oceans: temperate and tropical areas

Sloane's viperfish has long, fanglike teeth. It has a light-making organ that attracts prey in the darkness of the deep sea. Viperfish feed on smaller fish such as lanternfish.

Anglerfish

3¼ to 6½ feet
Coastal waters of Europe

The anglerfish has a spine on its head, tipped with a flap of skin. It lies on the seabed and moves the spine to attract other fish. When they come near, it opens its huge mouth and catches them.

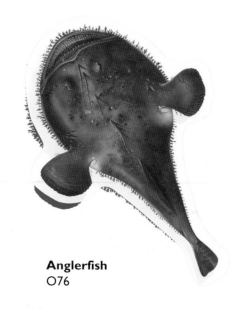

Anglerfish
O76

Shortnose batfish

11 inches
Caribbean

The shortnose batfish has a triangular body, flattened from top to bottom.

Longlure frogfish
O79

Sargassumfish

7½ inches
Atlantic, Indian, and Pacific Oceans: tropical areas

This fish is balloon-shaped and covered with bumps and flaps of skin. If it is attacked, it can pump itself into a ball, making it too big to swallow.

Shortnose batfish
O78

Longlure frogfish

6 inches
Tropical western Atlantic Ocean; Caribbean Sea

This fish has a rounded body and what looks like a fishing line on its snout.

Atlantic football fish

11 inches

23½ inches
All oceans

This deep-sea anglerfish attracts prey with the light on its head.

Linophryne

3 inches
Atlantic, Pacific, and Indian Oceans

The linophryne has a barbel on its chin that looks like a piece of seaweed. The end of it is luminous.

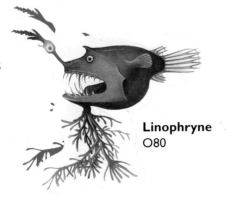

Linophryne
O80

Atlantic football fish
O81

35

Perchlike fish

This group of fish has more than 9,300 species, such as sea bass, cichlids, gobies, and wrasses. These fish have many different body shapes and include fish such as the barracuda, angelfish, swordfish, and Siamese fightingfish. All perchlike fish have one or two fins on their back, and most have pelvic fins close to their head. The pelvic fins usually have a spine and five rays.

Orange-throat darter
O82

Orange-throat darter

3 inches
Central U.S.

This little member of the perch family feeds on insects and plankton.

Perch
O83

Perch

14 to 20 inches
Europe

The perch lives in slow-moving water and feeds on fish. The fish breed in shallow water in spring. The females lay eggs in long strings that wind around plants or other objects.

Black grouper
O84

Black grouper

4 feet
Atlantic coastal waters;
eastern Gulf of Mexico

The black grouper weighs up to 50 pounds when fully grown. It has a large head and dark markings.

Greater amberjack

Up to 6 feet
Western Atlantic Ocean

The greater amberjack is a large fish with a sleek body and a deeply forked tail.

Greater amberjack
O85

Bluefish
O86

Bluefish

Up to 4 feet
Warm and tropical waters
of Atlantic, Indian, and western
Pacific Oceans

The bluefish is a fierce
hunter and kills more prey
than it can eat. It feeds
on any fish, including the
young of its own species.

Giant sea bass
O87

Giant sea bass

6½ feet
Pacific Ocean

This is a huge fish that can
weigh more than 550 pounds
and lives for over 70 years.

Florida pompano
O88

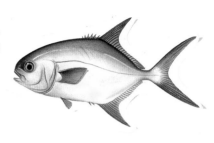

Florida pompano

20 to 26 inches
Western Atlantic Ocean

The pompano has a rounded
snout and a wide body,
which tapers sharply to a
forked tail. Its main food is
mollusks and crustaceans.

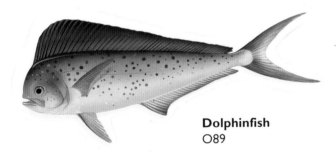

Dolphinfish
O89

Dolphinfish

Up to 5 feet
Warm and tropical waters of all oceans

This fish has a large fin along its back.
It moves in small schools and eats fish,
squid, and crustaceans.

Yellowtail snapper

30 inches
Western Atlantic Ocean, including Caribbean Sea

Snappers are common around coral reefs.
This species has a bright yellow tail and
a yellow stripe along each side.

Yellowtail snapper
O90

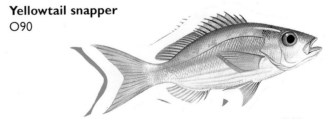

37

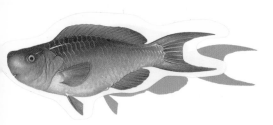

Blue parrotfish
O91

Clown anemonefish
O92

Queen angelfish
O93

Blue parrotfish

Up to 4 feet
Western Atlantic Ocean;
Caribbean Sea

This fish has beaklike jaws.
It eats algae, which it scrapes
from coral reefs with its teeth.

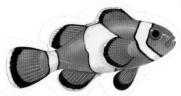

Clown anemonefish

3 inches
Pacific Ocean

This boldly striped fish lives
among the tentacles of large
sea anemones. It sometimes
cleans waste from its host.

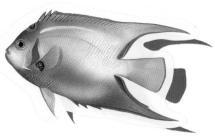

Queen angelfish

Up to 18 inches
Atlantic Ocean; Caribbean Sea

This colorful fish lives
among bright corals. It has
long fins on its back and
belly. Young queen angelfish
pick and eat parasites off
other fish.

**Copperband
butterflyfish**
O94

Copperband butterflyfish

8 inches
Indian and Pacific Oceans

This fish probes into crevices
in coral with its long,
beaklike snout to find food.

Sweetlip emperor

35 inches
Australia

This heavy-bodied fish
hunts for food around
coral reefs. Its name
may come from its
rather large lips.

Sweetlip emperor
O95

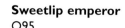
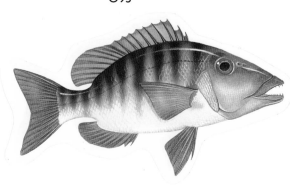

Scup

18 inches
Atlantic coast of North America

This fish has a forked tail
and spines on its fins. It eats
crustaceans and worms that it
catches on the seabed.

Scup
O96

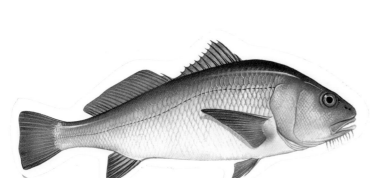

Red sea
bream
O97

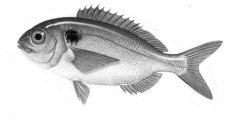

Red sea bream

14 to 20 inches
Atlantic Ocean;
Mediterranean Sea

This fish has a reddish
tinge to its body and fins,
and a dark spot above its
pectoral fin.

Black drum
O98

Black drum

4 to 6 feet
Western Atlantic Ocean

This large fish can weigh 150 pounds.
It eats mollusks and crustaceans, which
it crushes with flat teeth in its throat.
Oysters are a favorite food.

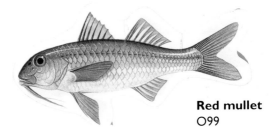

Red mullet
O99

Red mullet

16 inches
Eastern Atlantic Ocean; Mediterranean Sea

This fish finds food on the seabed using
the barbels on its chin. It changes color
to blend with its surroundings.

Tuna

Bigeye

Tuna can swim at speeds up to 50 miles an hour. They are streamlined in shape, with a pointed head and a body shaped like a torpedo. The 13 species of tuna live near the surface of warm and tropical oceans. All are hunters, feeding mainly on fish and squid. Many tuna swim in large schools, but the biggest fish swim in smaller groups or alone. Tuna must swim to breathe. Fish take their oxygen from the water that flows through their gills. Most fish have muscles to pump water over their gills, but not tuna. They have to keep swimming at all times to keep the water flowing over their gills.

Different sizes

The bluefin is the biggest and fastest tuna. It can grow to 10 feet long and weigh 1,200 pounds. The bigeye tuna can reach 7¾ feet, the smaller albacore 5 feet, and the smallest, the skipjack, 3 feet.

Skipjack

Bluefin

Albacore

Yellowfin

This tuna has long fins and yellow markings. It lives in the Atlantic and Pacific Oceans and can grow to about 6 feet long.

Yellowfin tuna are valuable food fish. Fishermen follow schools of yellowfin all over the world and catch large numbers.

Blue tang

12 inches
Western Atlantic Ocean;
Caribbean Sea

This fish has sharp spines on the sides of its tail that it raises to attack an enemy. The young are bright yellow with blue markings, but become blue all over when they are adult.

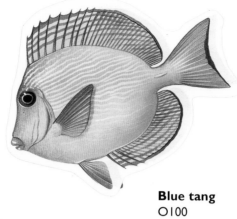

Blue tang
○100

Antarctic cod
○101

Antarctic cod

24 inches
Coastal waters of Antarctica

This is an icefish. It has a substance in its blood that allows it to survive at much lower temperatures than other fish. It eats mollusks, crustaceans, and worms.

Moorish idol
○102

Moorish idol

7 inches
Indian and Pacific Oceans

This fish has bold stripes and a long nose. It has a wide body and long, swept-back fins. Young fish have spines at the corners of their mouths. These drop off as the fish grows bigger.

Atlantic spadefish

18 to 36 inches
Western Atlantic Ocean

Young spadefish are black, but become silver with dark stripes down their sides as they grow up. They are often seen around shipwrecks.

Atlantic spadefish
○103

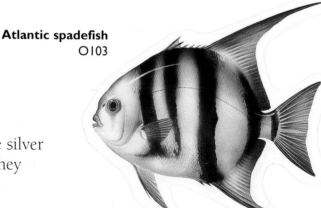

Dragonet

12 inches
Eastern Atlantic Ocean;
Mediterranean Sea

Dragonet
○104

The male dragonet has long blue-and-yellow fins. The female dragonet is smaller. Dragonets lie half-buried in the sand on the seabed, waiting to catch their prey.

Northern stargazer

Northern stargazer
○106

Up to 12 inches
Atlantic coast of North America

The northern stargazer has a large head with its mouth and eyes on top. This allows it to lie on the seabed with only its eyes and mouth uncovered.

Northern clingfish
○107

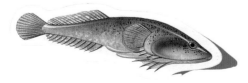

Northern clingfish

6 inches
Pacific Ocean

The northern clingfish has a smooth body and a wide head. It clings to rocks with a sucking disk on its belly. Its main food is mollusks and crustaceans.

Redlip blenny
○105

Redlip blenny

5 inches
Western Atlantic Ocean;
Gulf of Mexico; Caribbean Sea

This fish has a bristly nose, red lips, and a red-tipped dorsal fin. It lives on rocky seabeds. The female lays her eggs under rocks.

Rock goby

5 inches
North Atlantic Ocean;
Mediterranean Sea

The rock goby's pelvic fins form a sucking disk, which it uses to cling to rocks. It feeds on small invertebrates.

Rock goby
○108

Snakehead

3¼ feet
India; China; tropical Africa

Snakehead
O109

This long-bodied fish lives in tropical Africa and Asia. It has structures in its gills that help it take some oxygen from the air. It can even survive out of water, as long as it burrows into mud to keep its skin moist.

Siamese fightingfish
O110

Siamese fightingfish

2¼ inches
Thailand

The males of these freshwater fish fight over territory. In the breeding season, the male blows a bubble nest made of mucus. When the female lays her eggs, the male fertilizes them and spits them into the nest.

Man-of-war fish
O111

Man-of-war fish

9 inches
Tropical areas of Indian, Pacific, and western Atlantic Oceans

This fish lives among the tentacles of the Portuguese man-of-war jellyfish, but is not hurt by its stinging cells. The man-of-war fish probably removes parasites and other debris from its host's body.

Blue marlin

10 to 15 feet
Worldwide in tropical and warm seas

The blue marlin is one of the fastest fish and has a streamlined body and crescent-shaped tail. It weighs at least 400 pounds and has a long, beaklike nose.

Blue marlin
O112

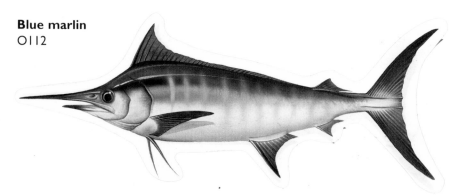

Atlantic mackerel

16 to 26 inches
Atlantic Ocean;
Mediterranean Sea

Atlantic mackerel
O113

Mackerel move in large schools and make regular journeys. In spring and summer they go north, where they breed. In winter, they return south again.

Swordfish

6½ to 16 feet
Worldwide in warm and tropical seas

The huge, spectacular swordfish is a fast hunter. It feeds on small fish and squid, and may use its very long snout to strike at schools of fish.

Swordfish
O114

Great barracuda
O115

Great barracuda

Up to 6 feet
Worldwide

The great barracuda has a long, slender body and large jaws. It is a fierce predator around coral reefs and has attacked people when disturbed. Young barracudas swim in schools.

Wahoo

Up to 6½ feet
Worldwide in tropical seas

The wahoo swims alone or in small groups. It has a narrow snout and many strong teeth. It can swim at speeds of up to 40 miles an hour when chasing prey.

Wahoo
O116

Sailfish

12 feet
Worldwide in warm and tropical seas

This fast-swimming fish has a fin like a sail on its back and long jaws. It is a fierce predator that eats squid and any kind of fish.

Sailfish
O117

45

Flying fish, lantern fish, and lizardfish

Most flying fish swim near the surface of the sea. They lift themselves into the air with their pectoral fins, then beat their tails fast to glide short distances. Lantern fish are deep-sea fish with light-making organs on their bodies. The lizardfish and the bummalo both live in shallow coastal waters.

Wrestling halfbeak
O118

Wrestling halfbeak

2¾ inches
Thailand; Malaysia

This small fish helps to control mosquitoes by feeding on their larvae.

Tropical two-wing flying fish

9 inches
All oceans

The flying fish escapes its enemies by leaping up and gliding over the surface of the water with the help of its fins.

Tropical two-wing flying fish
O119

Ballyhoo
O120

Lantern fish

4 inches
North Atlantic Ocean; Mediterranean Sea

This fish has light-making organs on its body. They help it find prey in the deep sea.

Lantern fish
O121

Ballyhoo

18 inches
Atlantic Ocean

This fish can skim over the surface of the water. It moves in schools, feeding on sea grass and small fish.

46

Red lizardfish
O122

Red lizardfish

12½ inches
Atlantic Ocean

The red lizardfish lies in wait for its prey on the seabed, then darts up and catches it in its sharp teeth.

Needlefish
O123

Needlefish

2 inches
South America

A long, slender body makes this tiny fish look like a dart. It uses its long lower jaw to scoop up plankton.

Bummalo
O124

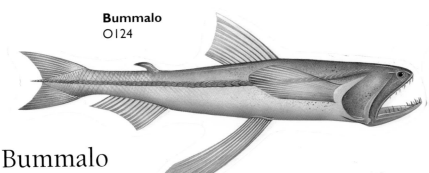

Bummalo

16 inches
Indian Ocean

The bummalo has a long body and huge jaws with sharp, curving teeth. It is often found near the mouths of large rivers.

Garfish
O125

Garfish

37 inches
North Atlantic Ocean;
Mediterranean and Black Seas

The slender garfish can live to be 18 years old. It is an active hunter and eats small fish and crustaceans. Garfish breed in coastal waters. Their small, round eggs stick to floating seaweed.

Atlantic saury

Atlantic saury
O126

16 to 20 inches
North Atlantic Ocean; Mediterranean Sea

Sauries swim in schools in surface waters, feeding on small fish and crustaceans. They have beaklike jaws.

47

Freshwater play

You can find the stickers of fish that live
on page 156. Stick them on this page to crea[t]
own freshwater scene.

Guppies, grunions, and relatives

Guppies belong to a large group of freshwater fish. Most are surface swimmers and feed on insects and plants. They can live in stagnant, slow-moving water. Grunions belong to a group that includes silversides, sand smelt, and rainbow fish. Most eat animal plankton.

Crimson-spotted rainbow fish

3½ inches
Australia; New Guinea

This colorful fish is one of about 53 types of rainbow fish found in Australia and New Guinea.

Crimson-spotted rainbow fish

Sand smelt

6 to 8 inches
Eastern Atlantic Ocean

This small fish swims in schools. It has a long, slender body and two fins on its back. Animal plankton is its main food.

Sand smelt
O128

Hardhead silverside
O129

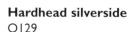
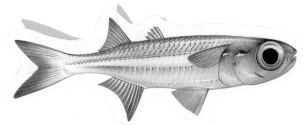

California grunion

California grunion
O130

7 inches
Pacific Ocean

Grunions swim ashore at night on a very high tide and lay their eggs in the sand. The next wave takes the fish back to the sea. Two weeks later, the eggs hatch and the young are carried out to sea.

Hardhead silverside

5 inches
North Atlantic Ocean

During the day, this little fish looks almost transparent, with a narrow, silvery stripe down each side. When night falls, its color darkens.

Four-eyed fish

12 inches
Central America;
northern South America

This fish has two eyes, each divided into two parts. The top part sees in the air and the lower part sees in water.

Four-eyed fish
0131

Sheepshead minnow
0132

Sheepshead minnow

3 inches
Atlantic coast of U.S.: Cape Cod south to Mexico

The female sheepshead lays her eggs and the male then fertilizes them. Sticky threads on the eggs help them stick to each other and to plants.

Mummichog

4 to 6 inches
North America

This is a hardy fish that can live in the sea or freshwater and eats almost any plants and animals it can find.

Mummichog
0133

Guppy

2¼ inches
Northern South America

The guppy helps to control mosquitoes by feeding on their larvae. It also eats small crustaceans and the eggs and young of other fish.

Cape Lopez lyretail

2¼ inches
Africa

The male lyretail is a colorful fish with large, pointed fins. The female is plainer.

Cape Lopez lyretail
0134

Guppy
0135

51

Squirrelfish, oarfish, and relatives

All these fish live in the sea. Squirrelfish, pinecone fish, roughie, and beardfish have spiny fins. Little is known about the oarfish and opah. The John Dory is part of another group of fish, many of which live in deep water. The whalefish is a deep-sea species.

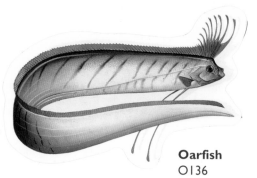

Oarfish
O136

Oarfish

23 feet
Atlantic, Pacific, and Indian Oceans: warm and tropical waters

This fish has a ribbonlike body and swims with rippling movements. It has no teeth in its small mouth.

Opah

6 feet
Worldwide, except Antarctica

This fish eats squid and fish such as hake and whiting. It has a large, round body with white spots and red fins.

Opah
O137

Stout beardfish

10 inches
Tropical areas of all oceans

This fish has a pair of whiskers, or barbels, hanging from its lower jaw. These may help it find food.

Squirrelfish
O138

Squirrelfish

24 inches
Atlantic Ocean

This brightly colored fish lives in coral reefs. It hunts at night for small crustaceans and other prey. Its large eyes help it see well in the darkness.

Stout beardfish
O139

Pinecone fish

5 inches
Indian and Pacific Oceans

The pinecone fish is covered in heavy, platelike scales. It has two light-making organs under its lower jaw.

Pinecone fish
0140

Roughie

12 inches
North Atlantic Ocean; south central Indian Ocean; Pacific near New Zealand

The brightly colored roughie has a large head and a wide body.

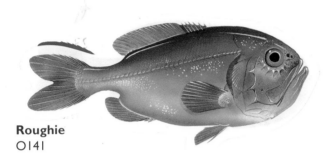

Roughie
0141

John Dory
0142

Whalefish

5½ inches
Indian Ocean

This is a small fish with a big name. It has a big head and no scales on its body. It seizes prey in its large jaws, which are lined with tiny teeth.

John Dory

16 to 26 inches
Eastern Atlantic Ocean; Mediterranean Sea

The John Dory is not a fast swimmer and catches its food by stealth. It approaches small fish and crustaceans slowly, until it is near enough to snap them up in its huge mouth.

Whalefish
0143

Gasterosteiformes

This group of bony fish includes some of the most unusual and strangely shaped fish. Sticklebacks and tubesnouts are spiny-finned fish that live in both the sea and freshwater. The weird pipefishes and sea horses live in shallow seawater. They cannot move quickly and rely on hiding from predators to survive.

Weedy sea dragon O144

Dwarf sea horse

1½ inches
Western Atlantic Ocean;
Caribbean Sea; Gulf of Mexico

This fish gently pushes itself along using its tiny dorsal fin. It can also attach itself to seaweed by curling its tail around it.

Dwarf sea horse
O145

Weedy sea dragon

18 inches
Coasts of southern Australia

The leaflike flaps of skin on this little sea horse help it to hide from its enemies among fronds of seaweed.

Three-spined stickleback

2 to 4 inches
Coasts and freshwater of North America

In the breeding season the male stickleback has a bright red belly. He makes a nest from tiny bits of plants glued together with mucus. He then attracts females to his nest.

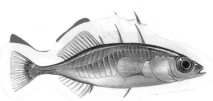

Three-spined stickleback
O146

Greater pipefish

12 to 19 inches
Eastern Atlantic Ocean: coasts of Norway to
North Africa; Mediterranean and Adriatic Seas

The body of the greater pipefish is covered
in bony armor. Its snout is long and tubular,
and has a small mouth at the tip.

**Greater
pipefish
O147**

Tubesnout

6¼ inches
Pacific Ocean: coast of
North America from Alaska
to Baja California

The tubesnout has a long,
cylindrical body that tapers
toward the tail. The small
mouth is at the tip of the
long snout.

Winged dragon

5½ inches
Indian and Pacific Oceans,
east Africa to north Australia

This fish has a flat body with
bony rings and a tapering tail.
Its snout is long and flattened,
with a small mouth underneath.

**Winged dragon
O148**

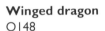

**Tubesnout
O149**

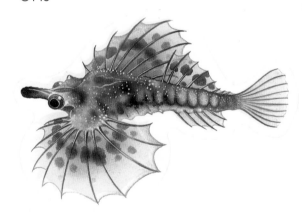

Shrimpfish

6 inches
Indian and Pacific Oceans to north Australia

The shrimpfish has a flat body with a sharp-
edged belly. At the end of its body is a long
spine. It often swims in an upright position,
with its snout held downward, pushing
itself along with its tail and anal fins.

**Shrimpfish
O150**

Flying gurnards and scorpionfish

The flying gurnard belongs to a small group of sea fish. Despite their name, these fish have never been seen flying above the surface of the sea. The scorpionfish group includes nearly 1,300 different species, most of which live in the sea. Many of these fish are chunky and spiny.

Flying gurnard

12 to 16 inches
Western Atlantic Ocean;
Mediterranean Sea

The flying gurnard uses its long pelvic fins to glide over the seabed as it searches for crustaceans to eat.

**Flying gurnard
O152**

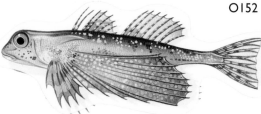

Lionfish

15 inches
Indian and Pacific Oceans

This extraordinary-looking fish has a brightly striped body and large, fanlike fins. The spines on its back are poisonous and can be dangerous even for humans.

Bullrout

10 to 24 inches
North Atlantic Ocean

This fish has spines near its gills and along each side. Females are usually larger than males. The bullrout lives on the seabed and eats crustaceans, as well as worms and small fish.

**Bullrout
O153**

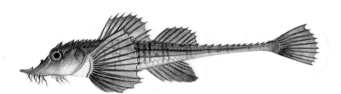

Stonefish
O154

Northern sea robin
O155

Northern sea robin

16 inches
Western Atlantic Ocean

The northern sea robin spends its life feeling for prey on the seabed.

Stonefish

12 inches
Indian and Pacific Oceans

The stonefish's mottled colors and irregular shape keep it well hidden as it lies among the stones on the seabed.

Redfish
O156

Redfish

32 inches to 3¼ feet
North Atlantic Ocean: Arctic to Scotland and Sweden;
U.S.: New Jersey

The redfish stays close to the seabed by day and rises to the surface at night to feed on herring and cod.

Sturgeon poacher
O157

Sturgeon poacher

Up to 12 inches
North Pacific Ocean: North American coast, Bering Sea to California

The sturgeon poacher has a body armor of bony plates. It has spines on its large head and clusters of barbels around its mouth.

Kelp greenling

21 inches
Pacific coast of North America: Alaska to California

The kelp greenling lives in the North Pacific. Its head is smooth and it has large pectoral fins and a notched dorsal fin.

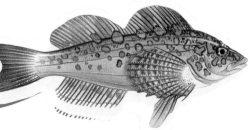

Kelp greenling
O158

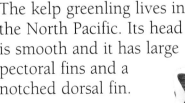

Flatfish

Most flatfish live in the sea. Young flatfish have rounded bodies, but as they grow their bodies flatten and the eye on one side moves so that both eyes are on the upper surface. The fish spends much of its life on the seabed, lying with its eyes facing up. Some flatfish have both eyes on the right side; others have them on the left.

Turbot

3¼ feet
Eastern Atlantic Ocean;
Mediterranean Sea

This broad-bodied flatfish varies in color and has speckled markings that help keep it hidden as it lies on the seabed. Adults feed mostly on fish, but the young eat small crustaceans.

Turbot
O159

Adalah

5 feet
Pacific Ocean

Some adalah have eyes on the left side, others on the right. But one eye is always on the edge of its head.

Adalah
O160

California halibut

Up to 24 inches
Red Sea; Indian Ocean;
western Pacific Ocean

This fish has a large mouth and strong, sharp teeth. A large halibut can weigh up to 70 pounds.

California halibut
O161

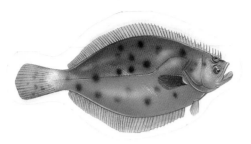

Summer flounder
O162

Naked sole

Up to 9 inches
Northwestern Atlantic Ocean

The naked sole has no scales on its skin and has dark stripes on its upper side. Its underside is whitish in color.

Naked sole
O163

Summer flounder

Up to 3¼ feet
Western Atlantic Ocean

The summer flounder feeds on crustaceans, mollusks, and fish, and will chase prey into surface waters.

Sole
O164

Sole

12 to 24 inches
Eastern Atlantic Ocean; Mediterranean Sea

The sole spends the day buried in sand or mud and feeds at night. It breeds in shallow water and the eggs float on the surface until they hatch.

Plaice
O165

Plaice

20 to 36 inches
Eastern Atlantic Ocean;
Mediterranean Sea

The top side of this flatfish is a rich brown color, dotted with orange spots. Both eyes are usually on the top—on the right side of the body.

Blackcheek tonguefish
O166

Blackcheek tonguefish

8 inches
Western Atlantic Ocean

This flatfish has eyes on the left of its head and its small mouth is twisted to the left side. It lives on the seabed.

59

Coelacanth, lungfish, and tetraodontiformes

The coelacanth is thought to look like some of the earliest fish. Lungfish are more closely related to amphibians than any other fish. Tetraodontiformes are spiny-finned fish. Their names—pufferfish, porcupine fish, boxfish, and triggerfish—give an idea of the strange body shapes of these fish.

Porcupine fish

36 inches
Tropical waters of Pacific, Indian, and Atlantic Oceans

This fish is covered with long spines that stand up when it is in danger, making it almost impossible to catch.

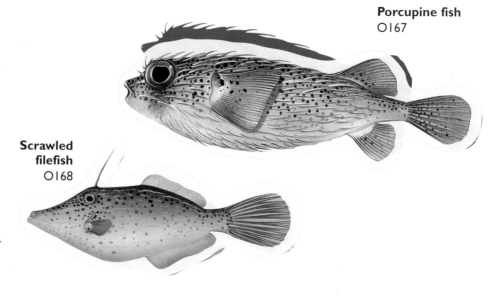

Porcupine fish
O167

Scrawled filefish

36 inches
Tropical waters of Atlantic, Pacific, and Indian Oceans

This fish has a long spine on its back and small, prickly spines on its scales. It eats invertebrates and seaweed, and feeds nose-down on the seabed.

Scrawled filefish
O168

Queen triggerfish

22 inches
Western Atlantic Ocean; Caribbean Sea

The triggerfish has three spines on its back. When in danger, it can wedge itself into a crevice by locking its spines. It feeds on small invertebrates.

Queen triggerfish
⚠ O169

Blue-spotted boxfish

18 inches
Indian and Pacific Oceans

This fish has a hard shell around its body, which protects it from its enemies.

Blue-spotted boxfish
O170

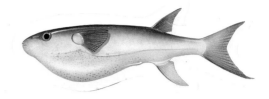

Pufferfish
O171

Pufferfish

24 inches
Tropical and subtropical Atlantic Ocean, occasionally as far north as Britain; Indian and Pacific Oceans

This pufferfish can fill its body with water, making the spines on its belly stand up.

Common puffer

6 inches
India; Myanmar; Malaysia

This fish can inflate its body until it is too fat for a predator to swallow.

Common puffer
O172

Sharpnose puffer

Sharpnose puffer
O173

4 inches
Atlantic Ocean

The sharpnose puffer is a stout, round-bodied little fish. It has a dark ridge along the middle of its back, and its head and body are scattered with blue markings.

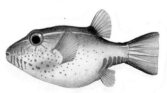

Coelacanth

Coelacanth
❗ O174

6¼ feet
Indian Ocean, off Comoro Islands

Coelacanths are heavy-bodied fish that feed mainly on other fish. The young fish hatch inside the mother before they are born.

South American lungfish

4¼ feet
Central South America

This lungfish lives in swamps that dry out for part of the year. During this time, it lives in a burrow dug in the mud and breathes air through lunglike organs. When it rains again, the fish comes out of its burrow.

South American lungfish
O175

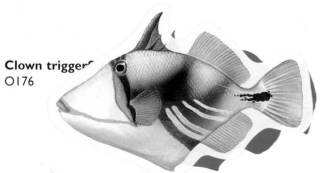

Clown trigger
O176

Clown triggerfish

13 inches
Indian and Pacific Oceans: east Africa to India, southeast Asia, north Australia, and Japan

The clown triggerfish has large spots on the lower half of its body. Its mouth is circled with bright orange and it has green markings on its back and tail fin.

Black-barred triggerfish

12 inches
Indian and Pacific Oceans: east Africa through southeast Asia to Hawaiian Islands

The black-barred triggerfish has dark and light bands running down its body. It can make loud sounds by rubbing together bones near its pectoral fin.

Black-barred triggerfish
O177

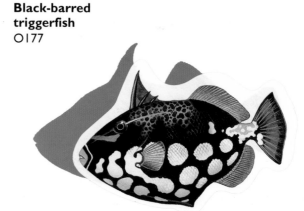

Scrawled cowfish
O178

Scrawled cowfish

18 inches
Western Atlantic Ocean: New England to Brazil,
including Gulf of Mexico and Caribbean

The scrawled cowfish is covered by a bony
shell. It has a pair of forward-pointing spines
on its head and a backward-pointing pair
near its tail.

Striped burrfish
O179

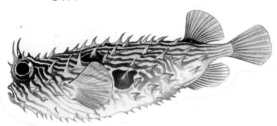

Striped burrfish

Up to 10 inches
Western Atlantic Ocean: Cape
Cod to Florida, south through
Gulf of Mexico to Brazil

The striped burrfish has an
oval body studded with fixed
thornlike spines.

Ocean sunfish

6 inches
India; Myanmar; Malaysia

The extraordinary ocean
sunfish is unlike any other
fish. Its body is almost
completely round and ends
in a curious frill-like tail.

Ocean sunfish
O180

Sargassum triggerfish

10 inches
Western Atlantic Ocean; tropical areas of
Indian and western Pacific Oceans

The sargassum triggerfish has dark, broken
stripes along its body. The young of this
species live under patches of floating seaweed.

**Sargassum
triggerfish**
O181

Deep-sea play page

You can find the stickers of fish and sea creat[ures that] live deep in the oceans on page 157. Stick the[m on this] page to create your own deep-sea scene.

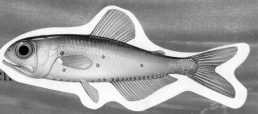

Sponges, jellyfish, and relatives

Sponges look more like plants than animals. Adult sponges stay in one place on a rock or the seabed. Sea anemones belong to a group of creatures called coelenterates, as do corals and jellyfish. Most have a tubelike body and stinging tentacles. Comb jellies are small animals that float in surface waters. Lampshells anchor themselves to rocks by a stalk.

Common comb jelly
O182

Common comb jelly

6 inches
Arctic and Atlantic Oceans

The comb jelly pushes itself though the water by moving the tiny hairs arranged in lines down its baglike body.

Vase sponge

Up to 20 inches
Caribbean Sea

Sponges are simple animals. To feed, they take water into their body, which traps and digests tiny pieces of food.

Vase sponge
O183

Portuguese man-of-war
O185

Lampshell
O184

Lampshell

1¼ inches
Atlantic Ocean

The lampshell has two shells and a short stalk on which it can move around. The shells open to expose folded tentacles.

Portuguese man-of-war

Float (head) 12 inches; tentacles 60 feet
Tropical waters in Atlantic, Indian, and Pacific Oceans

This creature is really a colony of hundreds of animals called polyps.

66

Brain coral
O186

Sea pen

Up to 15 inches
North Atlantic Ocean

The featherlike sea pen is a group of animals called polyps. One large, stemlike polyp stands on the seabed and supports the whole group.

Sea pen
O187

Brain coral

Colony up to 6½ feet wide
Indian and Pacific Oceans;
Caribbean Sea; southeastern
North Atlantic Ocean

This is a colony of tiny creatures called coral polyps. They create domed shapes that look like brains. The polyp skeletons form the rocky base of the colony.

Sea anemone

Up to 10 inches
Atlantic and Pacific Oceans

The sea anemone eats other sea creatures. It has a sucking disk under its body that holds onto a rock. The anemone's mouth has stinging tentacles around it.

Sea anemone
O188

Purple jellyfish

Bell 1¼ inches wide;
tentacles 36 inches long
Atlantic, Indian, and Pacific Oceans

This creature has stinging cells on its tentacles. These protect it from enemies and help it catch plankton to eat.

Purple jellyfish
O189

Crustaceans

There are thousands of species of crustaceans, including barnacles, crabs, lobsters, and shrimp. Wood lice live on land, and some shrimp species live in freshwater, but most crustaceans live in the sea. They have a tough outer skeleton that protects their soft body inside. The head has six segments, with two pairs of antennae and several different mouthparts. The rest of the body is divided into a thorax and an abdomen.

Deep-sea shrimp
0190

Deep-sea shrimp

4 inches long
Atlantic Ocean

The deep-sea shrimp's antennae are longer than its body. It spreads them out to find food in the deep sea.

Goose barnacle

6 inches, including stalk
Atlantic and Pacific Oceans

Goose barnacles fix their stalks to objects floating in the sea, such as logs, buoys, and boats. The barnacle's shell opens at the top.

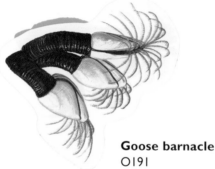

Goose barnacle
0191

Giant isopod
0192

American lobster

12 inches
North Atlantic coasts

This lobster hides during the day and hunts at night. It uses its huge pincers to crack and tear apart prey such as mollusks and crabs.

Giant isopod

5 inches
Antarctica

The giant isopod lives in Antarctic waters, where it catches any food it can find. It also scavenges on the seabed for dead and dying creatures.

American lobster
0193

Antarctic krill

Up to 2 inches
Antarctica

Shrimplike krill feed on plant and animal plankton that they sieve from the water. They are eaten by fish, penguins, and whales.

Antarctic krill
○194

Amphipod

Up to 1 inch
Atlantic and Pacific coasts

This small crustacean lives on the shore under rocks or seaweed. It has three pairs of jumping legs on its abdomen.

Amphipod
○196

Blue crab

9¼ inches wide
Atlantic and Gulf coasts of North America; South America to Uruguay; West Indies

The blue crab has five pairs of legs. The first pair has powerful pincers to break open the shells of prey.

Blue crab
○197

Hermit crab

Up to 4 inches
North Atlantic coasts

The hermit crab has no hard shell of its own. It protects its soft body by living in the empty shell of another creature, such as a snail.

Hermit crab
○195

Montague's shrimp

Up to 5 inches
North Atlantic coasts

Shrimp have much thinner shells than crabs or lobsters. They can swim with the limbs on their abdomen.

Montague's shrimp
○198

69

Mollusks

There are at least 100,000 living species of mollusks. The three main groups of mollusks are: limpets and snails; clams, mussels, and scallops; and squid, cuttlefish, octopuses, and nautiluses. In most mollusks the body is divided into three parts—the head, which contains the mouth and sense organs; the body; and a fleshy foot, on which the animal moves along. Most, but not all, mollusks have a tough shell that protects their soft body.

Butternut clam
O199

Butternut clam

6 inches
North Pacific Ocean

The clam lives in a burrow deep in a sandy or muddy seabed. It digs the burrow with its fleshy foot.

Iceland scallop

4 inches
Arctic and North Atlantic

The scallop has a soft body protected by two shells. It moves by pulling its shells together—this forces out jets of water, which push the mollusk along.

Iceland scallop
O200

Atlantic deer cowrie

Up to 5 inches
Western Atlantic Ocean;
Caribbean Sea

The cowrie is a type of sea snail that has a beautiful, shiny shell.

Atlantic deer cowrie
O201

Eastern oyster

Up to 4 inches
Atlantic and Gulf coasts
of North America

The oyster's soft body is protected by two hard shells. It eats tiny pieces of plant and animal food that it filters from the water.

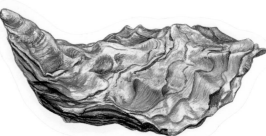

Eastern oyster
O202

Common octopus
O203

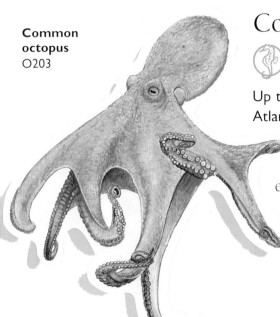

Common octopus

Up to 39 inches
Atlantic coasts

The octopus has a pouchlike body and eight long arms lined with two rows of suckers. It feeds on crabs, clams, and shrimp, which it kills with a poisonous bite.

Lightning whelk
O204

Lightning whelk

16 inches
Atlantic Ocean

This large whelk has a very beautiful shell with brown markings. It lives on seabeds in shallow water.

Chromodoris nudibranch
O205

Chromodoris nudibranch

6 inches
Pacific coasts

Nudibranchs, or sea slugs, are a group of snails that have no shells. They are often brightly colored.

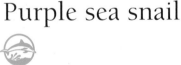

Purple sea snail
O206

Purple sea snail

1 inch in diameter
Atlantic, Indian, and Pacific Oceans

This little sea snail cannot swim, but drifts along on the surface of the sea, clinging to a raft of bubbles.

Longfin inshore squid

Up to 30 inches, including tentacles
Atlantic Ocean; Mediterranean Sea

The squid has suckers on its long tentacles to help it grasp fish and crustaceans.

Longfin inshore squid
O207

Rough periwinkle

The rough periwinkle lives on stones and rocks high up the shore.

Chiton

The chiton's shell has eight sections. When in danger, it can roll itself up like an armadillo.

Mollusks

Most sea creatures swim or float in the water, but some live attached to rocks or other surfaces. Barnacles live in large clusters on rocks. They begin life as larvae floating in the sea and feeding on plankton. Eventually, each barnacle finds somewhere to settle. It fixes itself to a rock with a cementlike substance, and does not move again. Limpets, periwinkles, and chitons all cling onto rocks with a suckerlike foot. This makes them hard to remove. Unlike barnacles, these creatures move around to graze on algae.

Acorn barnacle

At high tide, the barnacle opens its shell and puts out feathery arms to gather plankton to eat. When the tide is out, it keeps its shell top firmly closed.

Common limpet

A limpet leaves a sticky trail behind it when it moves. This helps it to find its way back after a feeding trip.

Common mussel

The mussel makes a sticky liquid inside its body and attaches the end to a rock to pull itself along. The shell is made of two halves, held tightly together.

Inside a mussel shell

Blue-rayed limpet

The blue-rayed limpet lives attached to seaweed. It eats seaweed fronds and small plants, such as algae, that grow on the seaweed.

Topshells are a kind of snail. They feed on tiny plants called algae and coral polyps. This topshell is surrounded by coral polyps.

Worms and echinoderms

There are about 11,500 species of worms. They include earthworms, which live on land, as well as some freshwater worms such as leeches, but most live in the sea. Echinoderms live in the sea. There are four main groups—brittle stars, starfish, sea cucumbers, and sea urchins. Most echinoderms move around using tiny stilts called tube feet, each tipped with a sucker.

Sea mouse
O208

Sea mouse

7 inches
Atlantic and
Mediterranean coasts

Despite its plump shape, the sea mouse is actually a kind of worm. It lives under mud or sand in shallow water.

Sea lily

Sea lily
O209

Up to 23 inches
Atlantic Ocean

This relative of the starfish lives attached to the sea bottom by a stalk. The sea lily's branching arms are lined with suckerlike tube feet.

Long-spined urchin

Body 4 inches wide; spines 4 to 15 inches long
Tropical parts of Atlantic Ocean; Caribbean Sea

Sharp spines protect this sea urchin's body from enemies. Its mouth is on the underside of its body and has five teeth arranged in a circle.

Brittle star

Brittle star
O210

Body 1 inch wide;
arms up to 4 inches long
Atlantic Ocean

The brittle star gets its name because its arms are easily broken off, although they grow back again.

Long-spined urchin
O211

74

Feather duster worm

5 inches
Atlantic Ocean; Caribbean Sea

The body of this worm is usually hidden in a tube made of sand. It catches food with its crown of feathery gills.

Feather duster worm
O212

Thorny starfish

5 inches across
Western Atlantic Ocean; Caribbean Sea

Large spines cover the body and arms of this starfish. It has two rows of tube feet on the underside of each arm.

Common sand dollar
O213

Common sand dollar

3 inches
North Atlantic and Pacific coasts

The sand dollar, a kind of sea urchin, has a shell covered with short bristles. It uses tube feet on the flat underside of its body to gather food as it moves through the sand.

Thorny starfish
O215

Sea cucumber

Up to 10 inches
North Atlantic Ocean

Sea cucumbers are related to starfish, but they have long, simple bodies. If threatened, the sea cucumber ejects sticky, white threads that confuse predators.

Sea cucumber
O214

Paddle worm

Up to 18 inches
Atlantic and Pacific coasts

This worm lives under rocks among seaweed, both on the shore and in deeper water.

Paddle worm
O216

Whales

Whales are the largest sea mammals. They have lungs, so they have to come to the surface regularly to breathe air. There are two kinds of whales: toothed and baleen. Baleen whales have bristly plates called baleen in their mouth, rather than teeth. When they feed, they take gulps of water. The baleen plates act like filters, so the water drains out but the fish or plankton stay in the whale's mouth. Toothed whales locate other sea creatures by sending out high-pitched clicking sounds and detecting the echoes as they bounce back from objects. Like most mammals, whales give birth to live young. A young whale is born underwater and is called a calf. As soon as it is born, the calf's mother helps it to swim to the surface so it can take its first breath.

Narwhal

13 to 20 feet
Arctic Ocean

The narwhal is related to the white whale but has only two teeth. One of the male's teeth grows into a spiral tusk up to 8 feet long, which sticks through its top lip. The tusk is probably used to impress females and fight other males in the breeding season. Females sometimes have a short tusk.

Narwhal
O217

White whale

13 to 20 feet
Arctic Ocean; subarctic waters

White whales, also called belugas, often live together in small groups called pods. They keep in touch with each other by making a variety of sounds, such as whistles, clicks, clangs, twitters, and moos. Polar bears prey on belugas that get trapped by the Arctic ice. In winter, big herds of belugas migrate south.

White whale
⚠ O218

Sperm whale

36 to 66 feet
All oceans

This toothed whale has a huge head filled with a waxy substance called spermaceti. This may help the sperm whale alter its buoyancy—its ability to float. This allows it to reach depths of more than 3,280 feet in search of squid to eat.

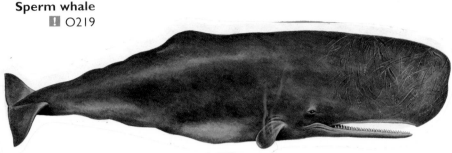

Sperm whale
❗ O219

Cuvier's beaked whale

21 to 23 feet
All oceans, temperate and tropical areas

The Cuvier's beaked whale has a tapering body and a long beak. Adult males have two teeth that stick out of their lower jaw. The coloring of this species varies from brown to gray or gray-blue.

Cuvier's beaked whale
❗ O220

Blue whale

82 to 105 feet
All oceans

The world's largest mammal, the blue whale can weigh up to 215 tons. This giant baleen whale feeds on huge quantities of tiny shrimplike creatures called krill, eating up to eight tons each day in the summer.

Blue whale
❗ O221

Humpback whale

48 to 62 feet
All oceans

The humpback whale is famous for the amazingly complex songs it sings to keep in touch with other whales and to attract mates. This baleen whale often sings for hours on end, pausing only to breathe. These songs travel great distances through the water.

Minke whale

26 to 33 feet
Temperate and polar areas of all oceans

This baleen whale is a smaller relative of the humpback and blue whales. In polar regions, the minke feeds mainly on krill, but in warmer waters it eats fish and squid as well.

Minke whale
O223

Sei whale
 O224

Gray whale

40 to 50 feet
Northeastern and northwestern Pacific Ocean

This whale stirs up the seabed with its snout and uses its baleen to filter out tiny creatures to eat. It makes a round trip of over 12,000 miles between its summer feeding waters off Alaska and the warmer, shallower waters off the coast of Mexico, where it breeds during winter.

Gray whale
O225

Sei whale

49 to 65 feet
All oceans, except polar regions

The sei whale is streamlined and flat-headed, so it can reach speeds of 26 miles an hour. It eats almost any kind of plankton, as well as fish and squid, usually feeding near the surface. Sei whales live in family groups of five or six, and pairs may stay together for many years. The young grow in their mother's body for a year before being born, and the calf is fed by its mother for six months.

Sowerby's beaked whale

16 to 20 feet
North Atlantic Ocean

There are a dozen closely related species of beaked whales. Most tend to live in deep water, staying clear of ships, so they are rarely seen and we know very little about them. All have fairly well-rounded bodies, with small flippers. Males are larger than females and have a small, pointed tooth at each side of their lower jaw. Females have smaller teeth.

Sowerby's beaked whale
O226

Dolphins and porpoises

Dolphins and porpoises are actually small, toothed whales. Dolphins are very friendly animals and move in groups. Porpoises are beakless whales. Like dolphins, they prey on fish and squid. Dolphins and porpoises have a thick layer of fat called blubber to keep them warm.

Dall's porpoise
O227

Harbor porpoise

4 to 6 feet
Northern Atlantic and Pacific Oceans;
Black and Mediterranean Seas

Porpoises feed on fish such as herring and mackerel. The female suckles her calf lying on her side on the water's surface so the calf can breathe easily.

Harbor porpoise
⚠ O228

Dall's porpoise

6 to 7 feet
Warm northern Pacific waters

These porpoises are larger than most porpoises and live in deeper waters. Groups of 100 or more porpoises, which are called schools, may migrate together.

Killer whale
O229

Killer whale

23 to 32 feet
Worldwide, especially cooler seas

The largest of the dolphin family, the killer whale, also called the orca, is a fierce hunter. It sometimes snatches seals from the shore or tips them off floating ice and into its mouth.

Ganges dolphin

5 to 8 feet
India; Bangladesh

The Ganges dolphin is one of only five species of freshwater dolphin. It lives in muddy rivers in southern Asia. It is blind and finds its food, fish and shrimp, by sending out high-pitched sounds and listening for the echoes.

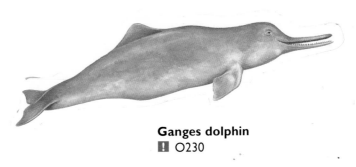

Ganges dolphin
❗ O230

Common dolphin
O231

Common dolphin

7 to 8 feet
Warm and tropical oceans worldwide

This beautifully marked dolphin lives in groups of between 20 and 100. They are often seen swimming alongside ships, leaping and rolling in the waves.

Bottlenose dolphin
O232

Bottlenose dolphin

10 to 14 feet
Warm and tropical oceans worldwide

The curving line of this dolphin's mouth makes it look as if it is always smiling. The bottlenose dolphin is often taught to perform tricks in aquariums in return for fish.

Above the surface

Our oceans, rivers, lakes, and wetlands also support a huge number of mammals, birds, reptiles, amphibians, and insects. These creatures rely on the water for finding food, or spend part of their lives in water, but live mainly above the surface.

Mammals that depend on water include seals, sea lions, otters, and hippopotamuses. Seabirds fly over the oceans searching for food, and come to land only to lay eggs. Crocodiles, alligators, turtles, and tortoises are all reptiles that divide their lives between land and water. Amphibians, such as salamanders, frogs, and toads, evolved from fish about 370 million years ago and still spend part of their lives in water.

These western gulls are flying off the coasts of California's Channel Islands. Gulls do not spend much time in the water, but they depend on the sea for their food. They eat fish, scavenge scraps from fishing boats, and take food from garbage dumps.

The Nile crocodile hatches out on land, but as an adult it will lurk underwater, waiting for prey.

Seals

Millions of years ago, the ancestors of seals left the land to live in the sea. Their bodies adapted to life in the water, becoming sleek and streamlined, and their limbs evolved into flippers for swimming. Because they have lungs, not gills like fish, they have to surface regularly to breathe. Unlike other sea mammals such as whales and dolphins, which give birth underwater, seals come ashore to have their babies.

Leopard seal

10 to 11 feet
Seas surrounding Antarctica

The leopard seal is the fiercest hunter of all seals. It has large jaws and teeth for grasping prey and tearing it apart. It hunts penguins by chasing and catching them underwater.

Leopard seal
O234

Harp seal

5 to 6 feet
North Atlantic and Arctic Oceans

Female harp seals form groups on the ice to give birth to their young. The pups grow very quickly as they feed on their mother's fat-rich milk.

South American fur seal

4 to 6 feet
Pacific and Atlantic coasts of South America

This seal eats fish, squid, and penguins. The female gives birth to a single pup. She stays with it for 12 days, then goes off to sea to feed, returning regularly to suckle her baby.

South American fur seal
O233

Harp seal
O235

Harbor seal

Harbor seal
O236

4 to 6 feet
North Atlantic
and Pacific Oceans

Like all seals, the harbor seal spends most of its life in the ocean. Harbor seal pups can swim from birth and dive for up to two minutes when just two or three days old.

Bearded seal
O237

Bearded seal

6 to 7 feet
Arctic Ocean

The bearded seal gets its name from the long bristles on its snout. It is a large species, and females are slightly longer than males. The female gives birth to a single pup, which can swim as soon as it is born.

Hooded seal

6 to 8 feet
North Atlantic Ocean:
Arctic and subarctic waters

Hooded seal
O238

Hooded seals spend much of their lives in open seas, diving deeply in search of food. They mainly eat fish and squid. The female has a single pup, which is born in the spring on floating ice and suckled for up to 12 days.

Northern elephant seal

Male up to 19 feet;
female up to 9 feet
Pacific coast of North
America: Vancouver Island
to Baja California

The elephant seal is named for its trunklike snout. It weighs up to 6,000 pounds.

**Northern
elephant seal**
O239

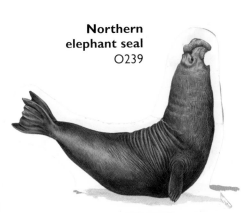

Antarctic seals

The continent of Antarctica is covered in thick ice, with temperatures as low as -128°F. Even the sea freezes over. However, several species of seal live there—the southern elephant, Ross, leopard, Weddell, crabeater, and South American fur seal. The southern elephant seal is the world's largest, weighing up to 8,800 pounds. For years, seals have been killed for their fur and blubber, and several species almost became extinct.

Crabeater seal

Crabeater seals feed on small, shrimplike creatures called krill, which they filter from the water through their teeth.

Elephant seal

A male southern elephant seal mates with a group of 40 to 50 females. If a rival male challenges him, he takes up a threatening pose, and the two seals may fight.

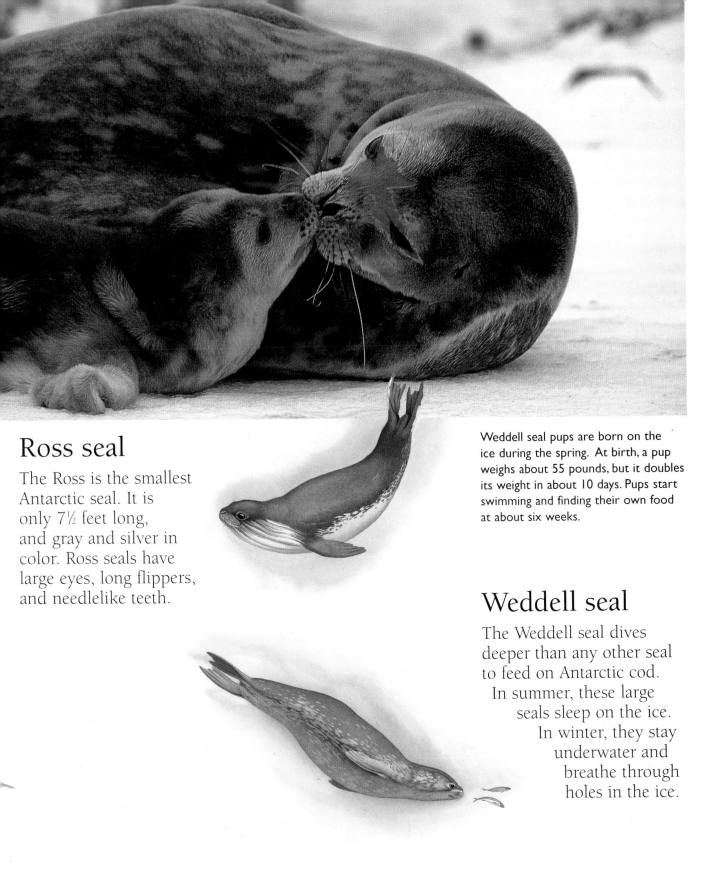

Ross seal

The Ross is the smallest
Antarctic seal. It is
only 7½ feet long,
and gray and silver in
color. Ross seals have
large eyes, long flippers,
and needlelike teeth.

Weddell seal pups are born on the
ice during the spring. At birth, a pup
weighs about 55 pounds, but it doubles
its weight in about 10 days. Pups start
swimming and finding their own food
at about six weeks.

Weddell seal

The Weddell seal dives
deeper than any other seal
to feed on Antarctic cod.
In summer, these large
seals sleep on the ice.
In winter, they stay
underwater and
breathe through
holes in the ice.

Sea lions, walruses, and sea cows

With their torpedo-like bodies, these marine mammals are skillful swimmers and divers. Sea lions and walruses are friendly animals and enjoy meeting in groups on coasts and islands. Sea cows (dugongs and manatees) are more closely related to elephants than to whales! They give birth underwater and then the mother helps the new baby to the surface to breathe.

Dugong

Up to 10 feet
Red Sea; Indian Ocean; waters off northern Australia

Dugongs and manatees are related to elephants. The dugong is large and fleshy, with a crescent-shaped tail. The female gives birth to a single baby and helps it to the surface to breathe.

American manatee

Up to 10 feet
Atlantic and Caribbean coastal waters from southeastern U.S. to Brazil

Manatees live in estuaries and shallow coastal waters. They are good swimmers and can reach speeds of 16 miles an hour. They use their tails as paddles and sometimes walk along the seabed on their flippers.

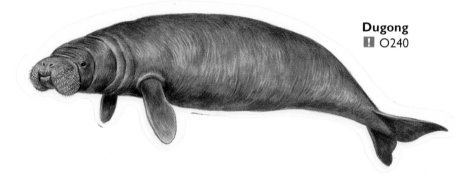

Dugong
⚠ O240

American manatee
⚠ O241

Walrus

7 to 11 feet
Arctic, North Atlantic, and North Pacific Oceans

Walruses live in the Arctic, where they feed on shellfish. They have long, sharp tusks, which they use for fighting and to drag themselves out of the water.

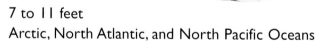

Walrus
O242

Californian sea lion

5 to 7 feet
Pacific coasts, from Canada to Mexico

This is the fastest swimmer of all the seals and sea lions, reaching speeds of 25 miles an hour. It also moves fast on land by turning its back flippers forward and lifting its body.

Californian sea lion
O243

Steller sea lion
■ O244

Steller sea lion

7 to 9 feet
North Pacific Ocean

This is the largest of the sea lions and it catches fish, squid, and octopus. A large male may even eat smaller seals such as fur seals. The Steller sea lion breeds in huge colonies.

Australian sea lion

Up to 8 feet
Off southern and southwestern Australian coasts and islands

This sea lion does not travel far from the beach where it was born. It often comes onto land throughout the year. It moves quite easily on land despite its large size.

Australian sea lion
O245

Other water-dependent mammals

These mammals all live in or near water. Even the hoofed mammals, such as the hippopotamus and water chevrotain, are good swimmers. The capybara, beaver, and swamp rat are rodents. They live near freshwater or swamps and eat waterside plants. The otter, water opossum, and platypus hunt for their prey in water and have webbed feet.

Sea otter
O246

American beaver
O247

Sea otter

Body 3 to 4 feet; tail 10 to 14 inches
Bering Sea, California

This otter feeds on shellfish and uses rocks to help it open the hard shells. The otter lies on its back in the water and bangs its prey against the rock until the shell breaks.

American beaver

Body 23 to 31 inches;
tail 7 to 12 inches
North America

One of the largest rodents, the beaver creates ponds by building dams across streams with branches and mud.

Capybara

Body 3 to 4 feet
Panama to eastern Argentina

The capybara has partly webbed feet and is an expert swimmer. When swimming, only its eyes, ears, and nostrils show above the water.

Capybara
O248

Platypus
O249

Platypus

Body 18 inches; tail 7 inches
Australia

The platypus feeds on riverbeds at dawn and dusk, using its sensitive bill to probe the mud for insects, worms, crayfish, and frogs.

Water opossum
O250

Swamp rat
O251

Water opossum

Body 10 to 13 inches;
tail 14 to 16 inches
Central and South America

This opossum has webbed hind feet and is the only marsupial that lives in water.

Swamp rat

Body 5 to 8 inches;
tail 2 to 7 inches
Southern Africa

The swamp rat often goes into water and can even dive to escape its enemies.

Hippopotamus
O252

Hippopotamus

Body 9 to 14 feet;
tail 14 to 20 inches
Africa, south of the Sahara

The hippo is one of the world's largest land mammals. It lives near rivers and lakes and spends up to 16 hours each day keeping cool in the water.

Water chevrotain

Body 29 to 33 inches;
tail 4 to 6 inches
Africa

The deerlike chevrotain is about the size of a hare and is a good swimmer.

Water chevrotain
O253

Seabirds

Life at sea is harsh and demanding for birds. Many seabirds, such as albatrosses, terns, and gannets, are powerful fliers. They cover long distances over the open ocean as they search for food. Some spend almost all their time in the air, coming to land only to mate, lay eggs, and raise their chicks. There are some seabirds, though, that cannot fly at all. Penguins are the best-known examples. They are expert swimmers and divers.

Dovekie
O254

Dovekie

8 inches
Arctic and North Atlantic Oceans; Bering Sea

Vast numbers of these birds, also known as little auks, live in the Arctic. Dovekies breed in colonies of millions on Arctic coasts and cliffs.

Snowy sheathbill

15½ inches
Antarctic coasts;
South Atlantic islands

Sheathbills eat any food they can find, including penguin eggs, chicks, and fish.

Snowy sheathbill
O255

Great black-backed gull
O256

Great black-backed gull

28 to 31 inches
Atlantic coasts of North America and Europe

One of the largest gulls, this bird is a fierce hunter. It chases and kills other seabirds, such as puffins.

Great cormorant

31 to 39 inches
Coasts of North America, Europe, Africa, Asia, Australia

The cormorant catches fish during underwater dives that may last as long as a minute.

Great cormorant
O257

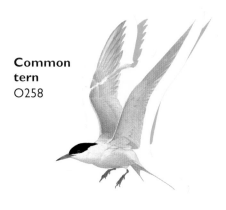

Common tern
O258

Common tern

13 to 16 inches
Eastern North America; northern Europe; Asia

A coastal bird, this tern feeds on shrimp and other small sea creatures. Terns nest in large colonies on islands and cliffs. The female lays two or three eggs in a nest on the ground.

Great skua

20 to 22 inches
North Atlantic Ocean

A strong bird with a hooked bill, the great skua is a fierce hunter. It steals other birds' food and kills seabirds and eats their eggs and young.

Great skua
O259

Herring gull

22 to 26 inches
Most of Northern Hemisphere

The herring gull is the most common gull on North American and European seacoasts. Herring gulls make a nest of grass on cliffs, islands, beaches, or rooftops.

Brown pelican

4 feet
Pacific and Atlantic coasts of North and South America

The brown pelican is the smallest pelican. It is a seabird and feeds by diving for fish, making high-speed plunges into the water from heights of more than 30 feet. In the water, it catches the fish with its beak.

Brown pelican
O260

Herring gull
O261

Little penguin

16 inches
New Zealand; southern Australia

The smallest of all the penguins, this species lives around coasts and islands. It nests in a crevice or burrow. The female lays two eggs, which both parents take turns incubating for up to 40 days.

Little penguin
O262

Galápagos penguin

20 inches
Galápagos Islands

The Galápagos penguin feeds mainly on small fish. It nests in small groups, and females lay two eggs in a cave or a hole in volcanic rock.

Red-tailed tropic bird
O263

Galápagos penguin
⚠ O264

Red-tailed tropic bird

36 to 40 inches, including tail
Indian and tropical Pacific Oceans

This elegant seabird is an expert in the air but moves awkwardly on land. It nests on ledges or cliffs to allow for easy takeoff.

Wandering albatross
⚠ O265

Wandering albatross

3½ to 4½ feet
Southern oceans

This seabird has the longest wingspan of any bird—up to 11 feet. It spends most of its life soaring over the open ocean.

African penguin O266

European storm petrel

5½ to 7 inches
Northeastern Atlantic Ocean
to the Mediterranean

The storm petrel spends most of its life at sea, only coming ashore to breed.

European storm petrel O267

African penguin

27 inches
South Africa

This penguin lives in a warmer climate than most other penguins. It is active on land only at night.

Atlantic puffin

11 to 14 inches
North Atlantic Ocean

The puffin can hold as many as a dozen fish at a time in its large, colorful beak.

Atlantic puffin O268

Northern gannet O269

Northern gannet

34 to 39 inches
North Atlantic Ocean
to the Gulf of Mexico

A sturdily built seabird with a strong beak, the northern gannet plunges 100 feet or more into the water to catch fish and squid.

Great frigate bird

34 to 40 inches
Indian and Pacific Oceans

This large seabird has a wingspan of more than 6 feet. It spends most of its life in the air. Large colonies nest on islands.

Great frigate bird O270

Beach play page

You can find the sticker ... ...nes
on pages 158–159. Stic...
your own beach scene.

Crocodiles and alligators

There are thirteen species of crocodiles, seven species of alligators and caimans, and two species of gavials. They are all large, armored reptiles that live both on land and in water. They are covered by hard scales for protection and are fierce hunters of other animals. Males and females look similar, but males tend to grow larger. Crocodiles and alligators have a pair of large teeth near the front of their lower jaw for grasping prey.

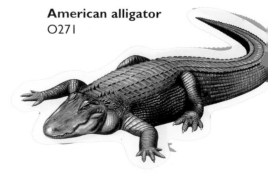

American alligator

Up to 23 feet
Southeastern U.S.

At one time American alligators became very rare because hunters killed so many for their skins. The species is now protected, and it has become more common. The female lays about 50 eggs in a mound of leaves, then guards the nest until the eggs hatch. The young stay with their mother for up to two years.

Gavial

Up to 18 feet
Southern Asia from Myanmar to Nepal and northern India

The gavial has long jaws containing about 100 small teeth—ideal for catching fish and frogs. It moves awkwardly on land and rarely leaves the water except to nest. The female lays 35 to 60 eggs in a pit that she digs with her back feet. She stays nearby for as long as three months until the eggs hatch.

Gavial
O272

Mugger crocodile

Up to 13 feet
Bangladesh; India; Iran;
Nepal; Pakistan; Sri Lanka

The mugger is a powerful
crocodile with a broad
snout. It can kill
mammals as large
as deer and buffalo,
but also eats
frogs, snakes,
and turtles.

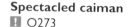

Spectacled caiman
⚠ O273

**Mugger
crocodile**
⚠ O274

Spectacled
caiman

5 to 6½ feet
Mexico to northern
South America

This caiman lives in any
watery habitat, including
those made by humans, such
as reservoirs and ponds. Like
many crocodiles, this species
has become rare, as so many
have been hunted and killed
for their skins.

**West African dwarf
crocodile**
⚠ O275

West African
dwarf crocodile

5 feet
Western Africa,
south of the Sahara

This crocodile has become
rare in recent years because
of changes to the rivers and
lakes where it lives, and
because of hunting. It is
active at night, when it feeds
on crabs, frogs, and fish.

Saltwater crocodile

Up to 27 feet
Southern India; Indonesia;
southern Australia

This is one of the largest
and most dangerous of all crocodiles. It has
been known to attack humans. It lives mostly
in the sea, catching fish, but it also kills land
animals such as monkeys, cattle, and buffalo.

**Saltwater
crocodile**
O276

99

Nile crocodiles

Unlike most reptiles, the female Nile crocodile is a good parent. After mating, she digs a pit near the river and lays 16 to 80 eggs. She covers the nest with soil, then both parents guard it for six to eight weeks until the eggs hatch. The mother may care for her young until they are six months old.

The crocodile's nest

The nest is made near water on a sandy beach or riverbank and is 7 to 17 inches deep. Once she has dug the nest burrow, the female lays her eggs inside.

Beginning life

When they are ready to hatch, the young crocodiles listen for any movements on the earth above them. When they hear their mother's footsteps, they call out. Once she has uncovered the nest, each baby uses the sharp egg tooth on its jaw to chip its way out of its shell. The mother may help to pull the babies free. Once the young crocodiles are out of the eggs, they must find shelter from the many predators waiting to catch them. The mother picks the babies up, a few at a time, and carries them in her mouth to a safe nursery site. She releases her babies in a quiet pool and defends them fiercely.

The Nile crocodile does not live only in the Nile River. It is found in rivers and lakes all over tropical and southern Africa. Adults can measure more than 16 feet long.

Fierce hunter

The Nile crocodile lurks in the water, often with only its eyes and nostrils showing. It drags prey into the water and drowns it.

Turtles

These armored reptiles have a hard shell to protect their soft body. Most turtles can pull their head inside the shell for protection. They have hard beaks instead of teeth for tearing off pieces of food. All turtles lay eggs. Most bury them in sand or earth and leave the hatchlings to make their own way out.

River terrapin

23 inches
Southeast Asia

A large, plant-eating turtle, the river terrapin lives in saltwater and rivers. It lays its eggs in sandbanks.

Pond slider
O278

River terrapin
❗ O277

Pond slider

5 to 12 inches
U.S.; Central America to Brazil

The pond slider rarely moves far from water. It often basks on floating logs. Young pond sliders feed mainly on insects and tadpoles, but as they grow they also eat plants.

Arrau River turtle

34 inches
Northern South America

This is the largest of the turtles known as sidenecks. These turtles pull their head into the shell sideways.

Arrau River turtle
O279

102

Wood turtle

5 to 9 inches
Eastern Canada;
northeastern
to midwestern U.S.

This rough-shelled turtle
stays near water but spends
most of its life on land.

Wood turtle
 ⬛ ○280

Matamata

16 inches
Northern South America

The unusual shape of this
turtle keeps it well hidden as
it lies among dead leaves on
the riverbed. Fleshy flaps at
the sides of its head wave
in the water and may attract
small fish.

Matamata
○281

Murray River turtle
○282

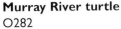

Murray
River turtle

12 inches
Southeastern Australia

Newly hatched Murray River
turtles have almost circular
shells. As they grow, the
shell becomes wider at the
back. Adult shells are oval.

Leatherback

5 feet
Tropical Atlantic, Pacific, and Indian Oceans,
but migrates to temperate waters

The world's largest sea turtle, the leatherback
weighs about 800 pounds. Its shell is not
covered with hard plates but is made of a
thick, leathery skin.

Leatherback
⬛ ○283

Common musk turtle

3 to 5 inches
U.S.

Also known as the stinkpot, this turtle produces a strong-smelling fluid if attacked.

Common musk turtle
O284

Spiny softshell
O285

Spiny softshell

5 to 18 inches
North America

Softshell turtles can move fast on land and in water but spend most of their lives in water. The spiny softshell feeds on insects, crayfish, and some fish and plants.

Loggerhead turtle

30 to 80 inches
Temperate and tropical areas of Pacific, Indian, and Atlantic Oceans; Mediterranean Sea

Loggerheads return to breed on the same beaches where they hatched. Females lay about 100 eggs in the sand.

Loggerhead turtle
❗ O286

Atlantic green turtle

3¼ to 4 feet
Tropical Atlantic, Pacific,
and Indian Oceans

This turtle spends most of its
life in the sea, and eats seaweed.
It may travel a long way to lay
its eggs on the beach where it was born.

Atlantic green turtle
❗ ○287

Alligator snapping turtle

14 to 26 inches
Central U.S.

This turtle can weigh up to 200 pounds.
It has a pink, fleshy flap on its lower jaw.
Any passing small creatures that come to
try this "bait" are quickly swallowed.

Alligator snapping turtle
❗ ○288

Hawksbill

30 to 36 inches
Tropical Atlantic, Pacific, and
Indian Oceans; Caribbean Sea

Hawksbills, which are sea turtles, have long
been hunted for their beautiful shells as well as
for their eggs. There are now strict controls on
hunting, but they are still very rare.

Hawksbill
❗ ○289

Caecilians, sirens, and mud puppies

Caecilians, sirens, and mud puppies are amphibians. Amphibians are "cold-blooded," which means they cannot control their own body temperature—some have to enter the water to cool down. Although most have lungs, amphibians gain much of the oxygen they need through their skin. Caecilians are wormlike amphibians. Some live in water for their whole lives, while others start their lives as water-dwelling larvae before moving onto land. Sirens and mud puppies are long-bodied amphibians with small, almost useless legs.

Sticky caecilian
O290

Sticky caecilian

Up to 15 inches
Southeast Asia

Adult caecilians live in burrows and feed on earthworms and small, burrowing snakes. They breed in the spring. The female lays 20 or more eggs in a burrow she makes in moist ground close to water.

Dwarf siren

4 to 10 inches
U.S.

The smallest of its family, the dwarf siren has no back legs and only tiny front legs.

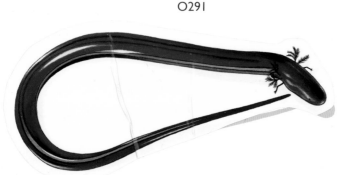

Dwarf siren
O291

Greater siren

20 to 38 inches
Southeastern U.S.

The siren has a long, eellike body. It has no back legs and swims by fishlike movements of its body.

Greater
siren
O292

106

Seychelles caecilian
O293

Seychelles caecilian

7½ inches
Seychelles

The Seychelles caecilian has a slightly flattened body that tapers at both ends. It burrows wherever the soil is moist. It often lives beneath rocks or logs or digs into rotting trees. It eats small invertebrates and frogs. Mating takes place at any time of year when there is plenty of rain. The young hatch as miniature adults.

Typhlonectes compressicauda

20 inches
Guianas; Brazil

This aquatic caecilian swims with eellike movements of its flattened tail. The female's eggs remain inside her body while the young develop. She then gives birth to live young.

Mud puppy

8 to 17 inches
Southern Canada; U.S.

The mud puppy spends all its life in water. It hunts worms, crayfish, and insects at night. The female lays up to 190 eggs, each stuck to a log or rock.

Typhlonectes compressicauda
O294

Mud puppy
O295

Salamanders and newts

Salamanders and newts are amphibians. A typical salamander or newt has a long body and tail and four legs. There are both water- and land-dwelling members of the order, but most stay near water. There are 350 different species of salmanders and newts.

Two-toed amphiuma

18 to 45 inches
Southeastern U.S.

The amphiuma lives only in water. It has a long body and tiny legs that are useless for walking. It hunts at night.

Olm
[!] O296

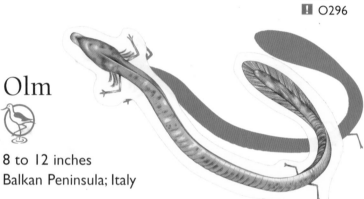

Olm

8 to 12 inches
Balkan Peninsula; Italy

This strange-looking salamander has a long body, a flattened tail, and small, weak legs. It is almost blind and lives in darkness in the streams and lakes of caves.

Two-toed amphiuma
O297

Rough-skinned newt

2½ to 5 inches
Western North America: Alaska to California

This is the most aquatic of Pacific newts. It has warty skin and small eyes with dark lower lids. It searches for its invertebrate prey both on land and in the water. Its toxic skin secretions repel most of its enemies. In the breeding season, the male's skin becomes smooth.

Rough-skinned newt
O298

Warty newt
O299

Warty newt

5½ to 7 inches
Parts of Europe; central Asia

The male of this large, rough-skinned newt grows a jagged crest on his back in the breeding season. Warty newts feed on small invertebrates, fish, and other amphibians.

Eastern newt

2½ to 5½ inches
Eastern North America

The young of this newt, which are called efts, leave the water when they are a few months old. They spend up to three years on land before returning to water.

Easte... newt
O300

Texas blind salamander

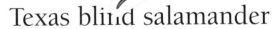

3½ to 5¼ inches
U.S.: southern Texas

The blind salamander lives in water in underground caves in total darkness. Its blood shows through its col...s skin, making it look pink. It ... dwelling invertebra...

Red salamander
O301

Red salamander

3¾ to 7 inches
Eastern U.S.

The brilliantly colored red salamander has a stout body and a short tail and legs. It lives mostly on land but usually stays near water.

Texas blind salamander
▯ O302

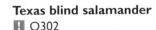

109

Spotted salamander

6 to 9½ inches
Southeastern Canada; eastern U.S.

Spotted salamanders spend most of their time alone and out of sight, burrowing through damp soil. But every spring they gather in large numbers around pools to mate and lay their eggs in the water.

Spotted salamander
O303

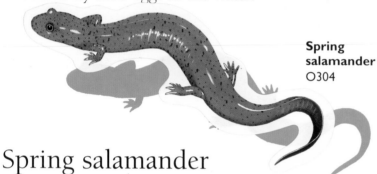

Spring salamander
O304

Spring salamander

4 to 9 inches
Southern Canada; U.S.: Maine to Georgia

The spring salamander spends most of its life in water, but on rainy nights it may come onto land to search for food.

Axolotl

Up to 11½ inches
Lake Xochimilco in Mexico

This salamander is now rare because so many have been caught for the pet trade. Many are also eaten by fish in the lake where they live.

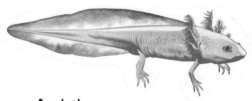

Axolotl
█ O305

Fire salamander

7 to 11 inches
Parts of Europe; southwestern Asia; northwestern Africa

Bright markings warn predators that this salamander's body is covered with an unpleasant-tasting slime.

Fire salamander
O306

110

Asian salamander

5½ inches
Japan

The female Asian salamander lays her eggs in water in sacs. Each sac contains 35 to 70 eggs. The male then takes the sacs and fertilizes the eggs but shows no interest in the female.

Asian salamander
O307

Sharp-ribbed salamander

6 to 12 inches
Portugal; Spain; Morocco

This salamander is one of the largest European amphibians. A powerful swimmer, it is usually active at night, when it searches for small invertebrate animals to eat. The female lays her eggs on a stone lying underwater.

Sharp-ribbed salamander
O308

Pacific giant salamander

2 to 11 inches
Northwestern North America

Most salamanders are silent, but this species makes a low-pitched cry. They live on land and are active at night.

Hellbender
O309

Hellbender

12 to 29 inches
U.S.

Despite its name, this large salamander is a harmless creature that hides under rocks in the water during the day. At night it hunts crayfish, snails, and worms, which it finds by smell and touch rather than by sight. The female lays up to 500 eggs on a streambed.

Pacific giant salamander
O310

Pond play page

You can find the stickers of insects, amphibians, and
reptiles that live near ponds and lakes on page 156.
Stick them on this page to create your own pond scene.

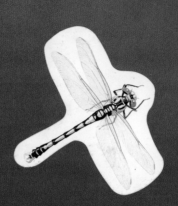

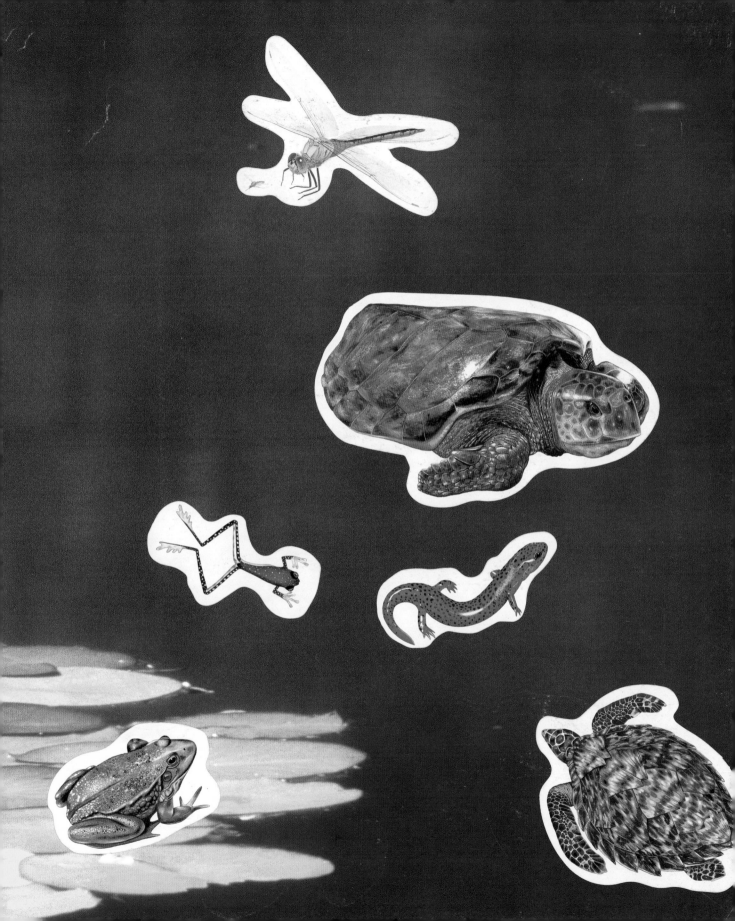

Frogs and toads

There are more than 3,500 species of frogs and toads. An adult frog or toad has long back legs, webbed toes, and no tail. The skin is either smooth or warty. Like all amphibians, frogs and toads are sometimes at home on land and sometimes in freshwater. Frogs and toads lay eggs that hatch into tailed, swimming young known as tadpoles. As the tadpoles grow, they develop legs, and they finally lose their tails when they are fully grown.

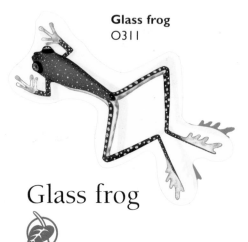

Glass frog
O311

Glass frog

Up to 1½ inches
Central America;
northern South America

This delicate little frog lives in small trees and bushes, usually near running water. It has sticky pads on its toes, which help it grip when climbing.

African clawed toad

2½ to 5 inches
Africa, south of the Sahara

This toad moves as fast in the water as any fish and can even swim backward. It uses its claws to dig in the mud around pools and streams for food. It eats any creatures it can find, even its own tadpoles.

African clawed toad
O313

Natal ghost frog
O312

Natal ghost frog

Up to 2 inches
Northeastern South Africa

This frog lives in fast-flowing mountain streams. The female lays her eggs in a pool. When the tadpoles move into the streams, they hold on to stones with their mouths to keep themselves from being swept away.

Cane toad

4 to 9½ inches
U.S.: southern Texas; Central and South
America; Africa; southern Asia; Australia

One of the largest toads in the world, the
cane toad makes a poisonous liquid that
may cause irritation and even death in
any mammal that tries to eat it.

Cane toad
O314

Midwife toad
O315

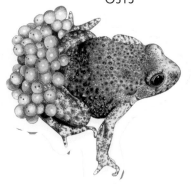

Oriental fire-bellied toad

2 inches
Siberia; northeastern China; Korean Peninsula

The brilliantly colored rough skin of the
fire-bellied toad gives off a poisonous milky
liquid that irritates the mouth and eyes of
any attacker. The female lays her eggs on
the undersides of stones in water.

**Oriental fire-
bellied toad**
O316

Midwife toad

Up to 2 inches
Western Europe; Morocco

The midwife toad hides by
day under logs. Unusually,
after the female has laid her
eggs, the male looks after
them, carrying them around
until they hatch.

Western spadefoot

1¼ to 2½ inches
Western U.S.; Mexico

An expert burrower, the western spadefoot
toad has a hard spike on each back foot that
helps it dig. It spends the day in its burrow
and comes out at night to feed.

**Western
spadefoot**
O317

Corroboree frog
⚠ O318

Gold frog

Up to ¾ inch
Southeastern Brazil

This tiny frog often lives among dead leaves on the forest floor but may also hide in cracks in trees or rocks in dry weather. It has a bony shield on its back and may use this to block off the entrance of its hiding place.

Gold frog
O319

Corroboree frog

1¼ inches
Australia

This frog lives on land near water and shelters under logs or in a burrow that it digs. The female lays up to 12 large eggs, which are usually guarded by one parent until they hatch.

Marsupial frog

Up to 1½ inches
Northwestern South America

The marsupial frog has an unusual way of caring for its eggs. The female carries her eggs in a skin pouch on her back for a few weeks, until they hatch into tadpoles.

Marsupial frog
O320

Amazon horned frog
O321

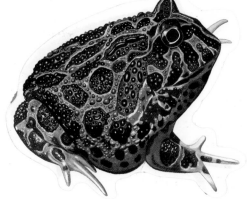

Amazon horned frog

Up to 8 inches
Northern and central South America

This horned frog is almost as broad as it is long and has a wide head and large mouth. It has a lump on each upper eyelid. It spends much of its life half-buried in the ground.

Darwin's frog
O322

Darwin's frog

1¼ inches
Southern Chile;
southern Argentina

This frog has unusual
breeding habits. The male
keeps the female's eggs in a
pouch under his chin until
they hatch into tadpoles.

Natterjack toad

2¾ to 4 inches
Western and central Europe

The male natterjack has the
loudest call of any European toad.
His croak carries a mile or more.
The natterjack usually lives on land
but is often found near the sea.

**Natterjack
toad**
O324

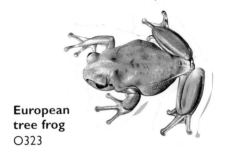

**European
tree frog**
O323

European tree frog

Up to 2½ inches
Central and southern Europe;
western Asia; northwestern Africa

This smooth-skinned frog
lives in trees. It can change
color very quickly, turning
from bright green in sunlight
to dark gray in shade.

Spring
peeper

¾ to 1¼ inches
Southeastern Canada;
eastern U.S.

**Spring
peeper**
O325

This agile frog can climb trees
and jump heights of more than
17 times its own body length.
In the breeding season, males
sit in trees calling to females
with a high-pitched whistle.

Arum lily frog

Up to 2¼ inches
Africa, mostly south of the Sahara

This frog changes color as
the light varies. In bright
sun it is light cream,
turning dark brown in
shade. It has sticky
pads on its toes to help
it grip as it climbs.

**Arum lily
frog**
O326

117

Red-banded crevice creeper

2 inches
Africa, south of the equator

Termites and ants are the main food of this frog. It digs in burrows or climbs trees to find insects. Its bright markings warn that it has poisonous skin.

Red-banded crevice creeper
O328

Wallace flying fro.
O327

Wallace's flying frog

4 inches
Sumatra; Borneo

This frog does not really fly, but uses its large, webbed feet and the flaps of skin on its front legs to help it glide from tree to tree.

Eastern narrow-mouthed frog
O329

Eastern narrow-mouthed frog

¾ to 1½ inches
Southeastern U.S.

A good burrower, this small frog can quickly disappear into the earth. It rests in a burrow during the day and comes out at night to hunt insects. It breeds in summer when there is heavy rain.

Marsh frog
O330

Marsh frog

Up to 6 inches
Central, southwestern, and eastern Europe; Morocco

This noisy frog spends most of its life in water, but comes out onto banks or lily pads. Males call night and day, particularly in the breeding season.

Mottled burrowing frog

Up to 1¼ inches
Africa, south of the Sahara

This frog has a small, pointed head, with a hard snout used for burrowing. The female lays her eggs in a burrow. When the young hatch, she digs a tunnel for them to swim to water.

**Mottled
burrowing frog**
O331

Northern leopard frog

2 to 5 inches
Most of northern North America, except the Pacific coast

This frog can live in any watery home and eats almost any creatures it can find. Each female lays about 5,000 eggs.

Northern leopard frog
O332

Bullfrog

3½ to 8 inches
Southeastern Canada; eastern and central U.S.; northern Mexico

The largest North American frog, the bullfrog spends most of its life in water. It is a good jumper and can leap nine times its own length.

European common frog

Up to 4 inches
Europe

Much of this frog's life is spent on land, feeding on insects, spiders, and other small creatures. It breeds in spring, when males attract females with their deep croaking calls. The females lay clusters of thousands of eggs.

**European
common
frog**
O333

Bullfrog
O334

Dragonflies, mayflies, and damselflies

Dragonflies, mayflies, and damselflies are all insects. Their young are called nymphs and live entirely underwater, in ponds or streams. As adults, these insects still stay close to water, hunting for smaller insects to eat. Dragonflies are fierce hunters and among the fastest-flying of all insects. They seize their prey in the air or pluck tiny creatures from leaves.

Biddy
O335

Damselfly

1¼ to 2 inches
Worldwide

These insects are sometimes known as spread-winged damselflies because they hold their wings partly spread out when at rest.

Damselfly
O336

Biddy

2¼ to 3¼ inches
Worldwide

Biddies are large dragonflies often seen around woodland streams, where they hover about 12 inches above the surface of the water. They are usually brownish in color and have big eyes.

Clubtail dragonfly
O337

Clubtail dragonfly

2 to 3 inches
Worldwide

The clubtail watches for its insect prey from a perch. Once it sights the prey, it darts out to seize it, then returns to the perch to eat it.

Mayfly
O338

Mayfly

½ inch
Temperate areas

Adult mayflies live for only one day—enough time to mate and lay eggs. Most of the mayfly's life, about a year, is spent in water as a nymph.

120

Narrow-winged damselfly

1 to 2 inches
Worldwide

The males of these damselflies are usually brighter in color than the females. The nymphs, like those of all damselflies, live in water and catch small insects to eat.

Narrow-winged damselfly
O339

Skimmer

¾ to 2½ inches
Worldwide

The skimmer dragonfly has a wide, flat body that is shorter than its wings. Some have a wingspan of up to 4 inches. Skimmers are usually seen flying near water.

Skimmer
O340

Darter
O341

Darter

¾ to 2½ inches
Worldwide

This dragonfly gets its name from its fast, darting flight. Like all dragonflies, darters lay their eggs in or close to water. The young live in water, catching prey like tadpoles.

Darner dragonfly
O342

Darner dragonfly

2¼ to 3½ inches
Worldwide

Darners are some of the largest and fastest of all dragonflies. When hunting, the darner zooms back and forth with its legs held ready to seize prey. The male patrols and defends an area against other males.

Glossary

amphibian A four-legged animal that can live both on land and in water.

bird A two-legged vertebrate that is covered with feathers and has a pair of wings.

extinction The complete dying out of a type of plant or animal.

gill The organ through which fish and other aquatic animals breathe underwater. As water moves through the gills, molecules of oxygen pass into the blood and are carried around the body.

habitat The natural home of an animal.

hoof The horny covering of the foot on a mammal.

incubate To supply eggs with heat for their development, often by sitting on them.

invertebrate An animal without a backbone. Creatures such as crabs, worms, and insects are all invertebrates.

larva The young form of many animals, particularly insects and amphibians, which develops into a different form as it grows.

lung The organ through which mammals and other land-living animals breathe the air.

mammal An animal that usually has hair on its body and feeds its young on milk produced in its own body.

marsupial An animal that continues growing in its mother's stomach pouch after birth.

predator An animal that hunts and kills other animals for food.

prey An animal hunted by a predator.

reptile A cold-blooded animal with lungs, a protective covering of scales, and babies born from eggs.

rodent A small mammal whose front teeth grow constantly and are gnawed down.

species A term for one type of plant or animal.

temperate Weather that is mild: neither tropical (hot) nor polar (cold).

vertebrate An animal with a backbone. Mammals, birds, reptiles, amphibians, and fish are all vertebrates.

warm-blooded Describes an animal, such as a mammal or bird, that can control its own body temperature. Most reptiles and amphibians depend on the sun's heat to warm their bodies and are said to be cold-blooded.

List of animals

A

adalah 58
albatross, wandering 94
alewife 22
alligator, American 98
amberjack, greater 36
amphipod 69
amphiuma, two-toed 108
anemonefish, clown 38
angelfish, queen 38
anglerfish 34

B

ballyhoo 46
barnacle, goose 68
barracuda, great 45
beardfish, stout 52
beaver, American 90
bichir 20
bigmouth buffalo 25
blackcheek tonguefish 59
bluefish 37

bowfin 20
boxfish, blue-spotted 61
brain coral 67
bream 25
    red sea 39
brittle star 74
bullrout 56
bummalo 47
burbot 32
burrfish, striped 63
butterflyfish, copperband 38

C

caecilian
    Seychelles 107
    sticky 106
caiman, spectacled 99
candirú 26
capybara 90
carp, common 24
cascarudo 26
catfish
    Australian freshwater 26
    blue 27
    glass 27
    sea 27
    walking 27
char, Arctic 31
chevrotain, water 91
chromodoris
        nudibranch 71
clam, butternut 70
clingfish, northern 43

cod
    Antarctic 42
    Atlantic 33
coelacanth 61
cormorant, great 92
cowfish, scrawled 63
cowrie, Atlantic deer 70
crab
    blue 69
    hermit 69
crevice creeper, red-banded 118
crocodile
    mugger 99
    saltwater 99
    West African dwarf 99

D

damselfly 120
    narrow-winged 121
darter, orange-throat 36
dolphin
    bottlenose 81
    common 81
    Ganges 81
dolphinfish 37

dovekie 92
dragon, winged 55
dragonet 43
dragonfly
 biddy 120
 clubtail 120
 darner 121
 darter 121
 skimmer 121
drum, black 39
dugong 88

E

eel
 conger 23
 European 23
 New Providence cusk 32
 snipe 23
 spiny 23
elephant-snout fish 21

F

fightingfish, Siamese 44
filefish, scrawled 60
flying fish, tropical two-wing 46

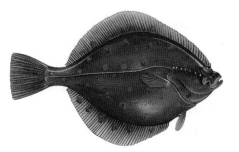

four-eyed fish 51
frigate bird, great 95
frog
 Amazon horned 116
 arum lily 117
 bullfrog 119
 corroboree 116
 Darwin's 117
 eastern narrow-
  mouthed 118
 European common 119
 European tree 117
 glass 114
 gold 116
 marsh frog 118
 marsupial 116
 mottled burrowing 119
 natal ghost 114
 northern leopard 119
 spring peeper 117
 Wallace's flying 118
frogfish, longlure 35
flounder, summer 59

G

gannet, northern 95
gar, longnose 20
garfish 47
gavial 98
goby, rock 43
goldeye 21
goldfish 24
grayling 31

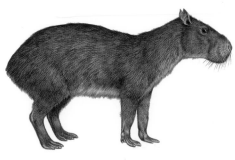

greenling, kelp 57
grenadier, rough-head 32
grouper, black 36
grunion, California 50
gull
 great black-backed 92
 herring 93
guppy 51
gurnard, flying 56

H

haddock 33
hagfish, Atlantic 13
halibut, California 58
hatchetfish 34
herring, Atlantic 22
hippopotamus 91

I

isopod, giant 68

J

jelly, common comb 66
jellyfish, purple 67
John Dory 53

K
krill, Antarctic 69

L
lampshell 66
lamprey, sea 13
lantern fish 46

ling 32
lionfish 56
lizardfish, red 47
lobster, American 68
lungfish, South
          American 62
lyretail, Cape Lopez 51

M
mackerel, Atlantic 45
man-of-war fish 44
man-of-war, Portuguese 66
manatee, American 88
manta ray, Atlantic 13
marlin, blue 44

mayfly 120
minnow, sheepshead 51
Moorish idol 42
moray, Mediterranean 23
mud puppy 107
mullet, red 39
mummichog 51

N
needlefish 47
newt
    eastern 109
    rough-skinned 108
    warty 109

O
oarfish 52
octopus, common 71
olm 108
opah 52
opossum, water 91

otter, sea 90
oyster, eastern 70

P
pacu 24
paddlefish 21
parrotfish, blue 38
pearlfish 33
pelican, brown 93
penguin
    African 95
    Galápagos 94
    little 94
perch 36
petrel, European storm 95
pinecone fish 53
pipefish, greater 55
piranha, red 24
pirarucu 21
plaice 59
platypus 91
pollock, walleye 33
pompano, Florida 37
pond slider 102
porcupine fish 60
porpoise
    Dall's 80
    harbor 80
puffer
    common 61
    sharpnose 61
pufferfish 61
puffin, Atlantic 95

R

rainbow fish, crimson-
    spotted 50
rat, swamp 91
ray, electric 12
redfish 57
redlip blenny 43
roach 25
robin, northern sea 57
roughie 53

S

sailfish 45
salamander
    Asian 111
    axolotl 110
    fire 110
    hellbender 111
    Pacific giant 111
    red 109
    sharp-ribbed 111
    spotted 110
    spring 110
    Texas blind 109
salmon
    Atlantic 31
    sockeye 31
sand dollar, common 75
sand smelt 50

sardine 22
sargassumfish 35
saury, Atlantic 47
sawfish, greater 13
scallop, Iceland 70
scup 39
sea anemone 67
sea bass, giant 37
sea cucumber 75
sea dragon, weedy 54
sea horse, dwarf 54
sea lily 74
sea lion
    Australian 89
    Californian 89
    Steller 89
sea mouse 74
sea pen 67
sea snail, purple 71
seal
    bearded 85
    crabeater 86
    elephant 86
    harbor 85
    harp 84
    hooded 85
    leopard 84
    northern elephant 85
    Ross 87
    South American fur 84
    Weddell 87
shark
    basking 14
    bluntnose six-gilled 17

    common saw 17
    Greenland 17
    hammerhead, smooth 15
    horn 16
    mako 14
    monkfish 17
    nurse 16
    Port Jackson 14
    sandy dogfish 15
    thresher 14
    whale 16
    white 15
    wobbegong 15
sheathbill, snowy 92
shrimp
    deep-sea 68
    Montague's 69
shrimpfish 55
silverside, hardhead 50
siren
    dwarf 106
    greater 106
skate 12
skua, great 93
Sloane's
    viperfish 34
snakehead 44
snapper,
    yellowtail 37
sole 59
    naked 59
spadefish,
    Atlantic 42
sponge, vase 66

squid, longfin inshore 71
squirrelfish 52
starfish, thorny 75
stargazer, northern 43
stickleback,
     three-spined 54
stingray, southern 12
stonefish 57
sturgeon, Atlantic 21
sturgeon poacher 57
sunfish, ocean 63
surubim 26
sweetlip emperor 38
swordfish 45

tropic bird, red-tailed 94
trout, rainbow 31
tubesnout 55
turbot 58

W
wahoo 45
walrus 88
wels 27
whale
     blue 77
     Cuvier's beaked 77
     gray 79
     humpback 78
     killer 80
     minke 78
     narwhal 76
     sei 79
     Sowerby's beaked 79
     sperm 77
     white 76
whalefish 53
whelk, lightning 71
white sucker 25
worm
     feather duster 75
     paddle 75
wrestling halfbeak 46

T
tang, blue 42
tarpon 22
tench 25
tern, common 93
terrapin, river 102
toad
     African clawed 114
     cane 115
     midwife 115
     natterjack 117
     Oriental fire-bellied 115
     western spadefoot 115
triggerfish
     black-barred 62
     clown 62
     queen 60
     sargassum 63

turtle
     alligator snapping 105
     Arrau River 102
     Atlantic green 105
     common musk 104
     hawksbill 105
     leatherback 103
     loggerhead 104
     matamata 103
     Murray River 103
     spiny softshell 104
     wood 103
typhlonectes
     compressicauda 107

U
urchin, long-spined 74

Acknowledgments

ARTWORK CREDITS
Fish
Robin Boutell, John Francis, Elizabeth Gray, Colin
Howard, Colin Newman, Guy Smith, Michael Woods

Mammals
Graham Allen, John Francis, Elizabeth Gray,
Bernard Robinson, Eric Robson, Simon Turvey,
Dick Twinney, Michael Woods

Birds
Malcolm Ellis, Keith Brewer, Hilary Burn, Steve Kirk,
Colin Newman, Denys Ovenden, Peter David Scott,
Ken Wood, Michael Woods

Reptiles & Amphibians
John Francis, Elizabeth Gray, Steve Kirk, Alan Male,
Colin Newman, Eric Robson, Peter David Scott

Insects
Colin Newman, Michael Woods

Habitat Symbols
Roy Flookes

PHOTOGRAPHIC CREDITS
8–9 David B. Fleetham/ Oxford Scientific Films;
28–29 NOAA Central Library; **41** Richard Herrmann/
Oxford Scientific Films; **48–49** NOAA Central Library;
64–65 Marshall Editions; **73** Pal Kay/ Oxford Scientific
Films; **82–83** Amox Nachoum/ Corbis; **87** Rick Price/
Oxford Scientific Films; **96–97** Global Book Publishing;
112–113 Robert Harding Photo Library

Place these stickers on the shapes that match these animals. **Find** them on pages **77–79**.

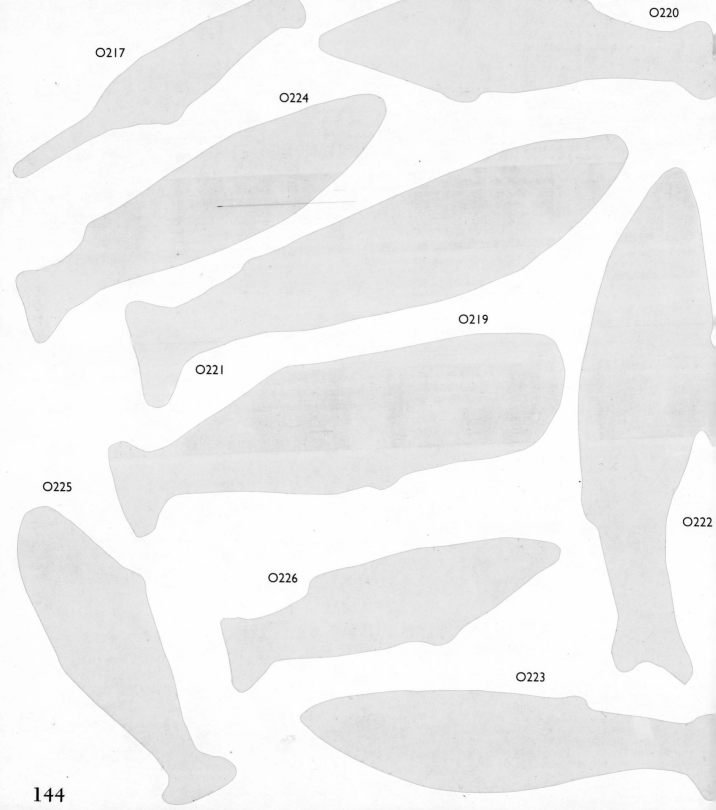

O220

O217

O224

O219

O221

O225

O222

O226

O223

Place these stickers on the shapes that match these animals. **Find** them on pages **80–81** and **84–85**.

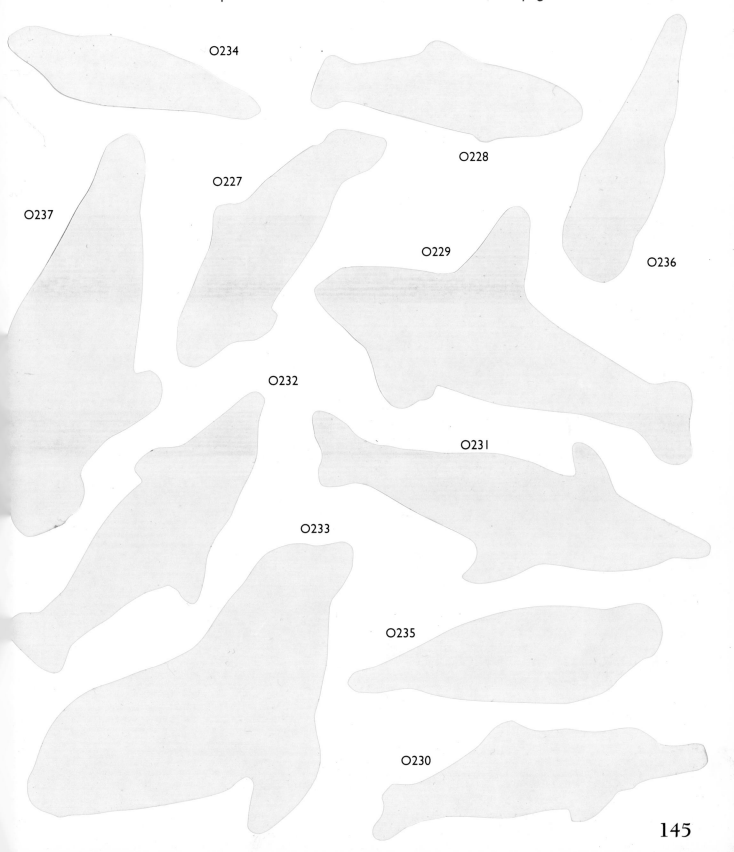

O234

O228

O227

O237

O229

O236

O232

O231

O233

O235

O230

145

Place these stickers on the shapes that match these animals. Find them on pages 85 and 88–90.

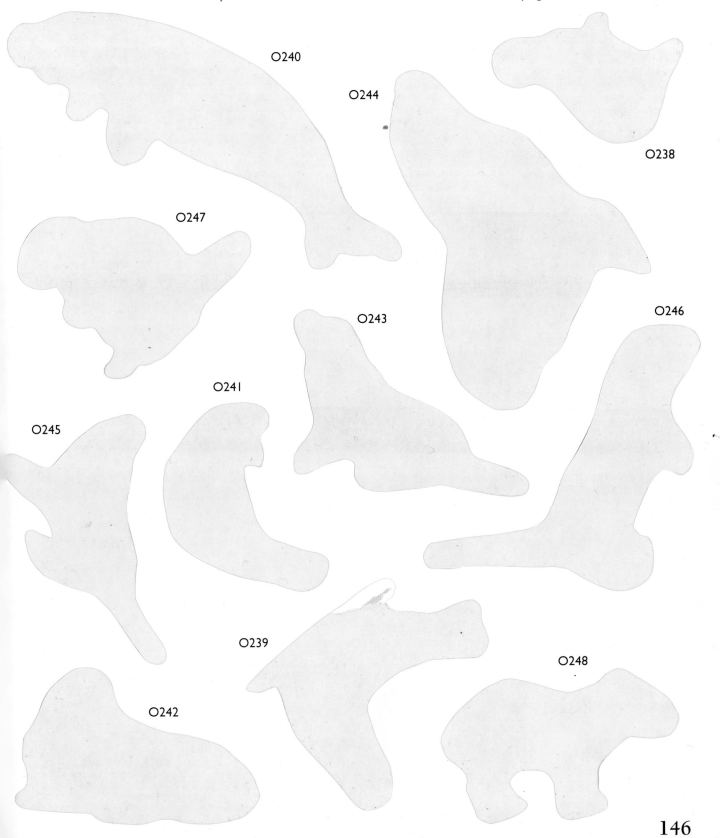

O240

O244

O238

O247

O243

O246

O241

O245

O239

O248

O242

Place these stickers on the shapes that match these animals. **Find** them on pages **91–94**.

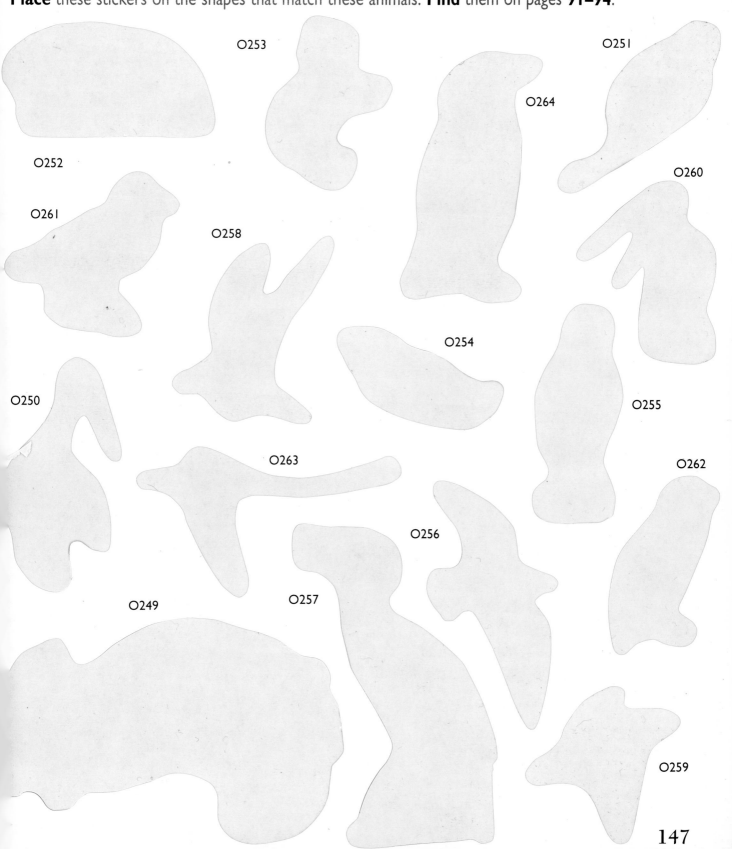

O253

O251

O264

O252

O260

O261

O258

O250

O254

O255

O263

O262

O256

O257

O249

O259

Place these stickers on the shapes that match these animals. **Find** them on pages **94–95** and **98–99**.

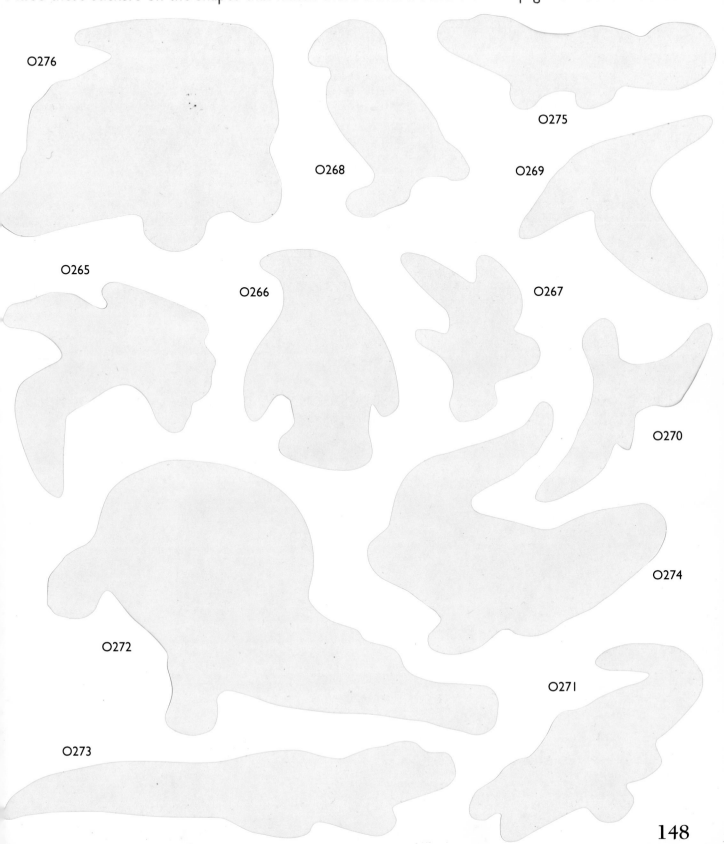

O276

O268

O275

O269

O265

O266

O267

O270

O274

O272

O271

O273

Place these stickers on the shapes that match these animals. Find them on pages 102–104.

O284

O280

O285

O277

O279

O282

O278

O286

O281

O283

149

Place these stickers on the shapes that match these animals. **Find** them on pages **105–107**.

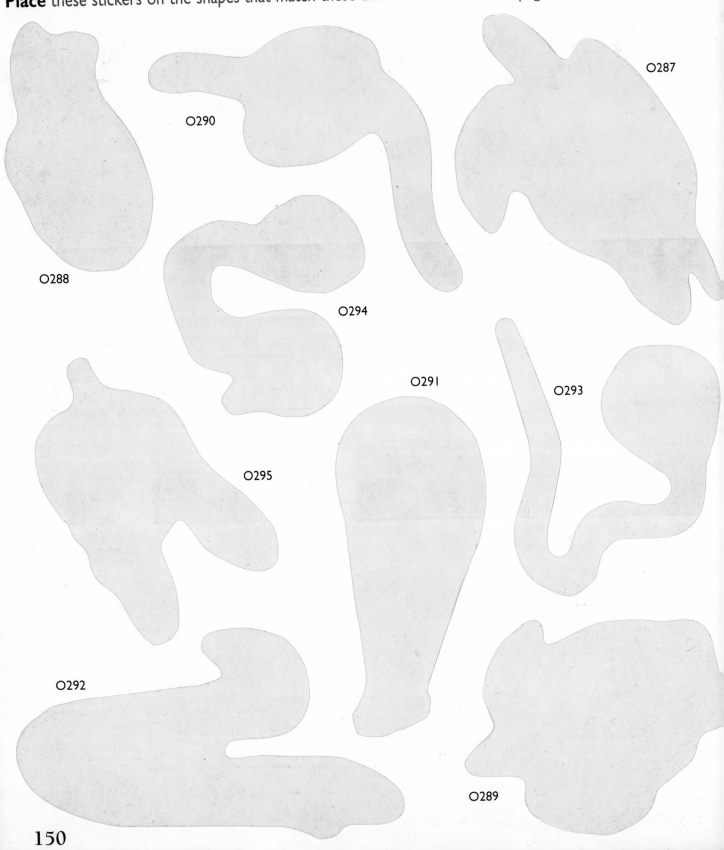

O287

O290

O288

O294

O291

O293

O295

O292

O289